Local Perspectives on Globalisation: The African Case

Local Perspectives on Globalisation: The African Case

RESEARCH ON POVERTY ALLEVIATION

Mkuki na Nyota Publishers
P.O. BOX 4246, Dar es Salaam, Tanzania

Published for:
Research on Poverty Alleviation (REPOA)
P.O. Box 33223, Dar es Salaam, Tanzania by

Mkuki na Nyota Publishers
P.O. Box 4246, Dar es Salaam, Tanzania.

REPOA   ISBN 9987-615-00-7
Mkuki na Nyota Publishers   ISBN 9976-973-89-6

Contents

INTRODUCTION

Joseph Semboja, Juma Mwapachu and Eduard Jansen

This introduction does not aim to provide a detailed synthesis of the debate on globalisation. Its main purpose is to provide a general framework of the central issues that feature in detail in the papers published in this volume.

Definition

How to define globalisation is in itself a subject of some contention. There is, however, significant consensus that globalisation constitutes the rapidly increasing complex interactions between societies, cultures, economies, technologies, governance, institutions and individuals worldwide. Its critical dynamic is the compression of time and space, while it dramatically shifts and stretches relationships from local to global contexts. Its power and momentum is derived from growing market capitalism and global advances in communications technologies.

Global society is in the throes of a momentous change at almost all levels: social, economic, political and cultural. Globalisation basically sums up, in a word, the character of this change. Much has been written during the past decade on this state of radical transformation. However, the focus has predominantly been on global perspectives, in particular on the new realities about the global economy and the resultant impacts at local nation-state levels. A recent notable departure is 'The Case Against the Global Economy and for a Turn Towards the Local' by Jerry Mander and Edward Goldsmith.

It is this case for a turn toward the local that inspired the international workshop on 'Local Perspectives on Globalisation' held in Dar es Salaam, Tanzania, on 10-11 September 1998 and the subsequent publication of this book.

Impact

Globalisation is not a new phenomenon, but its dynamics may have changed over time. In Africa, the slave trade, the partitioning of the continent, colonial governance, externally imposed economic systems (encouraging production for export and import for consumption) and the Cold War were all part of the globalisation process. The consequences of many of these important historical events are well documented.

More recent development thinking has favoured the market and the private sector-driven economy and has promoted the liberalization and deregulation of economies and governance at a time when technological developments have also significantly reduced natural cross-border barriers. This environment has given fresh impetus to the globalisation process. There is little doubt that globalisation has produced significant gains at the global level. However, the evidence shows that these gains have been concentrated in a few developed countries, leaving the majority to share the brunt of the costs.

The Gains

At the global level, globalisation has facilitated the growth of foreign trade, including the movement of goods and services, capital, technology and labour. This has in turn promoted economic growth and human advancement in the participating economies. Between 1980 and 1997, international trade in goods and services increased threefold, with exports and imports growing at about the same rate. At the same time, increased foreign investments, expanding media and internet connections facilitated the transfer of technology and provided opportunities for reduction in productivity differences. From 1990 to 1997, foreign direct investments (FDI) grew twofold at the global level.

In addition to economic gains, significant benefits have accrued in the domains of culture and governance. Public awareness in the areas of human rights, democratic rights, gender rights, etc. has increased significantly due to enhanced accessibility to newspapers, radio, television, telephone, computer and internet. Foreign news is no longer the monopoly of the state or of the privileged social and economic groups.

The Reality

Countries gain from globalisation when they take advantage of easier access to capital markets, information and technology, and of the improved competitive environment, which enables them to exploit their comparative advantages. These opportunities lead to improved allocative efficiency for growth, human development and poverty reduction. However, experience has shown that the process of globalisation produces both winners and losers. And, although some countries (e.g. in Africa) have largely been losers, many others have shifted from being losers to winners, or vice versa. Several reasons have been given as to why some countries have become losers. We group them into three areas:

1. Not all markets are free, as is the dominant belief within globalisation thinking. Specifically, the labour market has remained segmented. Unskilled labour continues to be immobile due to barriers imposed by governments in industrialized countries. Skilled labour, on the other hand, tends to flow from the poor countries to the rich ones. This imbalance has produced a number of effects. First, since goods and services produced by skilled labour have high value and greater mobility, exports in the rich countries have grown more quickly. In other words, globalisation is a greater catalyst for the faster movement of goods produced in developed countries. Second, since capital and technology are more effective complements to skilled than to unskilled labour, the transfer of technology to poor countries has failed to produce the expected results. This weakness has been exacerbated further by a rigid intellectual property rights regime which has tended to favour the rich countries. As a consequence, productivity and earnings differences across and within poor countries have tended to widen.

2. High transaction costs – associated with location (e.g. landlocked countries), poor infrastructure, undeveloped financial banking and capital market systems, low level technology, inadequate skills, inadequate contract enforcement, an inadequate legal system, inadequate enforcement of existing laws, corruption, bureaucracy, etc. – lower the productivity of both labour and capital and promote their outflow. Evidence abounds in this regard that Africa has a high level of brain drain and capital flight.

3. The losers have not produced adequate exportables. During the

periods 1980-1990 and 1990-1998 global GDP grew at 3.2% and 2.4% per year respectively. The corresponding percentages for East Asia and the Pacific, South Asia and Sub-Saharan Africa were 8.0% and 8.1%, 5.7% and 5.7% and 1.8% and 2.2%, respectively. Taking account of the average annual population growth rate of 5% and 3%, Sub-Saharan Africa's per capita GDP actually declined during the two periods. As a result of this growth during the two periods, global exports grew at 5.2% and 6.4% per year. The corresponding percentages for East Asia and Pacific, South Asia and Sub-Saharan Africa were 9.6% and 14.0%, 6.6% and 10.5% and 2.4% and 4.6%, respectively. Therefore, although Sub-Saharan Africa remained highly integrated in the world economy with an export-GDP ratio of 33% in 1980 and 30% in 1998 (compared to 20% and 25% for the entire world, 21% and 34% for East Asia and Pacific and 8% and 13% for South Asia), it was increasingly becoming an insignificant contributor to global trade. The contribution of Sub-Saharan Africa to total exports fell from 3.8% in 1980 to 1.5% in 1997, compared to an increase from 4.6% to 9.6% for East Asia and Pacific and a rise from 0.1% to 1.0% for South Asia.

The Costs

There are many costs associated with the process of globalisation. Here we deal with a few, and group them into four areas.

1. The level of inequality between the rich and poor countries has increased rapidly in recent years. The income gap between 20% of the world population living in the rich countries and 20% living in the poorest countries increased from 30:1 in 1960 to 60:1 in 1990 and to 74:1 in 1997. These trends will continue at a faster rate as the flow of capital, new technology, skilled labour and information continue to favour the industrialized world. By the late 1990s, 20% of the world's population living in rich countries controlled 68% of the world's FDI compared to only 1% controlled by 20% living in the poorest countries. In the area of communications, the percentages were 74% against 1.5% for telephone lines and 93% against 0.2% for internet users (UNDP, 1999: 2-3). A similar situation is observed in research and development, patent applications and ownership, ownership of

radios, television sets and personal computers (UNDP, 1999: 3 and World Bank, 1999: 267).

2. There is a rapid increase in the level of income inequality in the loser countries. Globalisation favours skill-intensive, modern (and usually large and capital-intensive) sector activities. The weak linkage between modern and informal sector activities prevents the transfer of knowledge and the equalisation of productivity between the two sectors, thereby promoting inequality of earnings. In addition, globalisation favours market-oriented sectors and activities and completely ignores those oriented towards subsistence production.

3. The rapid depletion of natural resources and environment is taking its toll. The lack of comparative quantitative information precludes a thorough and accurate review of the state of natural resources and the environment. Only a few examples can be given to illustrate the situation. Between 1990 and 1995, for instance, the global annual rate of deforestation was estimated to be around 20 square kilometres per one million inhabitants. The corresponding rate for East Asia and Pacific, South Asia and Sub-Saharan Africa was 19, 1 and 58 km/one million people respectively. For Tanzania, it was 124 (World Bank, 1999 Tables 3 and 9). While Tanzania's sustainable supply of fuel wood is estimated to be 19 million cubic metres per year, consumption is estimated at 43 million cubic metres per year. In addition to deforestation, poor countries face a number of natural resource and environmental problems that are worth mentioning here. In Tanzania, for example, the following situation prevails:

⟨ The (near) extinction of some animal and plant species. Both *anonidium usambaratensis* and *saint paulia megunsis* plants, for instance, have recently disappeared.

⟨ The rapid deterioration of grazing land capacity. In some livestock-dependent areas in Dodoma, Singida, Shinyanga and Arusha regions livestock keepers now require 12 hectares to feed one cow.

⟨ Increased accumulation of solid waste in the urban areas. Only about 10-20% of solid waste is treated and disposed.

⟨ Increased urban water pollution. 80% of urban dwellers use

pit latrines and 5% have no toilet facilities of any kind.
⟨ Illegal trade in Appendix One animals, such as chimpanzees and elephants.

Obviously these are unsustainable costs. Nevertheless, the problem will continue and may even accelerate given the lack of government capacity to formulate policies or enact new legislation to protect natural resources and the environment, or to enforce existing legislation. What is worse is that the globalisation process creates an incentive system that works against the preservation of natural resources and the environment.

4. The erosion of national control over governance and culture. Clearly, globalisation also has positive consequences in this area, and these have been acknowledged. However, a number of significant negative consequences have emerged. Irresponsible politicians have used corrupt methods to buy votes, leading to adverse outcomes. Personal insecurity has also increased as criminals have engaged in illicit trading in drugs and weapons. HIV/AIDS is rampant. Widespread fundamentalism across religions has not only increased social tension and insecurity, but has also had adverse economic effects as solutions to social and economic problems are sought in prayer rather than hard work. Increasing family tensions arise as marriages break up, children rebel, poverty strikes and incurable diseases consume the most productive elements in society.

In short, globalisation has unleashed a hybrid system of culture, governance and economics that is neither local nor foreign and whose institutional framework has yet to be developed and grasped, and the capacity to manage it developed.

Contributions

This publication brings together some of the leading thinkers in Africa and abroad to reflect upon globalisation. In a nutshell, all the papers show that the complexities of globalisation make it too difficult for poor countries to grasp the process, let alone to develop the capacity for its management. Although much of the current debate on globalisation focuses on its new form, for Africa – as mentioned above – the process started many years earlier with the slave trade, the partitioning of the continent, colonial governance, externally determined economic systems and the manoeuvrings of the Cold War. In other words, the new form of globalisation is different only in its dynamics. In both cases, Africa has been and continues to be the most vulnerable. The various papers in this volume explain this phenomena from different perspectives. The papers and the discussions during the workshop raise concerns about the erosion of African culture and identity as a result of the increasing domination of global over national governance and the increased accessibility of global media instruments. The economic and political implications of this erosion also form an interesting part of the debate. In spite of the imbalance in development that arises from globalisation, there is broad consensus about its inevitability and that poor countries have no choice but to develop strategies that enable them to reverse the imbalance. The papers and the discussions call for more proactive intervention by the various national stakeholders – especially government but also the private sector and NGOs – in the globalisation process. However, due to the complexities surrounding the process, the participants in the workshop felt that a major research effort was needed to clarify the form of the intervention.

The papers that form part of this publication can be summarized as follows. In his speech opening the workshop, Matthew Luhanga emphasizes the importance of brainpower as a key determinant in managing the globalisation process. He raises several questions regarding the role of higher education in the production of appropriate brainpower. Ademola Oyejide, through a review of literature, outlines the economic benefits and costs of globalisation and how Africa has performed over the last two decades. Brian van Arkadie tackles the subject from a historical perspective, arguing that the main problem in the East African region is not as much 'excessive integration into the world economy' as the "lack of integration" *ab initio*. This conclusion is also reached by Oyejide. Van Arkardie also sees the importance of learning from the past (including the colonial period), other countries (especially East Asia) and selected local business community participants (especially Asians) to inform policies and strategies for greater national integration into the world economy. A comprehensive review of literature on the economic domain of globalisation by Samuel Wangwe and Flora Musonda discusses the implications of globalisation at the local level, especially in promoting trade, investment and technology. They review the roles of various institutions and stakeholders at the national, regional and global levels in preparing national economies to meet global economic challenges. Jenerali Ulimwengu points out that globalisation has always produced 'globalizers' and 'globalizees'. In his view, developing countries and Africa in particular have been globalized throughout modern history. He argues strongly for the role of the state in regulating the process of globalisation and protecting citizens against any damage caused by it. He also sees a positive role for regional groupings, civil society and good leadership in promoting national economic agendas. Issa Shivji's paper brings to the fore an interesting aspect of popular resistance. He argues that coping mechanisms or forms of resistance may be expressed in different forms – institutionally and methodologically – and that they may not be formal or even documented. Indeed, they have largely remained under-researched. Penina Mlama, having defined culture to be 'a people's way of life', proceeds to show how, as a result of globalisation, the African way of life can no longer be identified with Africa; how behavioural patterns, ideas, beliefs, values, attitudes, and institutions are now simply a hybrid resulting from global interactions. She goes on to argue that this loss of identity and independence has had a negative impact on the political and economic life of the globalized nations. Finally, Idris Kikula and Aida Kiangi discuss the implications of natural resources trading in an environment of inadequate capacity and lack of will to implement policies and legislation. This, they argue, may have led to over-exploitation of specific species, some of them nearing extinction.

Lastly, it is important to note that all the presentations acknowledged the complexities introduced by globalisation and the challenge they pose to nations at the level of policy and strategy formulation. The papers see the important role of national institutions in promoting the interests of citizens in the globalisation process. More specifically, they underscore the role of the state. Clearly though, the complexities involved call for further and deeper research to support policy interventions. Most of the papers offer suggestions for areas of future research.

It is our hope that the discussions encapsulated in this publication will offer the reader some insight into the underlying thesis on giving globalisation a local perspective. The world is indeed on the edge; but should Africa be allowed to fall off?

References

Mander, Jerry and Goldsmith. Edward (1996), *The Case Against the Global Economy and for a Turn Towards the Local.* Sierra Club Books, San Francisco.

UNDP. (1999), *Human Development Report 1999.* Oxford University Press, New York.

World Bank (1999), *World Development Report 1999*, Oxford University Press, New York.

OPENING SPEECH

Prof. M.L. Luhanga
Vice-Chancellor,
University of
Dar es Salaam

Mr. Chairman,

It is perhaps better to start by agreeing on a definition of the word 'globalisation'. The organizers of this workshop define globalisation as '...the rapidly increasing complex interactions between societies, cultures, institutions and individuals worldwide. Its critical dynamic is the compression of time and space, while it dramatically shifts and stretches relationships from local to global contexts'.

Globalisation as defined above could not have occurred without major advances in transportation systems and in information and communication technologies. Faster and more reliable surface and air transportation systems, high bandwidth fibre-optic and satellite communication systems and powerful computers have combined to shrink time and space making it possible for closer and more intense interactions to take place at a global level.

Globalisation has many dimensions, some of which are covered by the papers to be presented at this workshop. Broadly speaking, globalisation may be said to be occurring in the economic, social, cultural and political dimensions, with the economic dimension receiving the most attention.

This preoccupation with the economic dimension of globalisation has its roots in history. During the late 1920s and early 1930s there was a series of worldwide financial crashes that ultimately spiralled down into the Great Depression. As GNPs fell, the dominant economies created trading blocs (the Japanese Co-Prosperity sphere, the British Empire, the French union, Germany and Eastern Europe, and the USA with its Monroe Doctrine) to minimize imports and protect jobs. The restrictions on imports increased the downward pressure on all countries and worsened the depression.

In the aftermath of the Second World War the GATT-Bretton Woods trading system was set up to prevent a repetition of these events. Trade restrictions and tariff barriers were gradually reduced in a series of trading rounds (such as the Kennedy round and the Tokyo round) culminating in the formation of the WTO.

Our preoccupation with the economic dimension should not blind us to the importance of the social, cultural and political dimensions of globalisation. Indeed these dimensions are crucial to the efficient and effective functioning of national economic systems and the global economic system. I note with appreciation that the workshop agenda contains papers which will address these issues.

This workshop's main focus is on exploring the need for research in the field of globalisation and in particular its impact at the local level. I wish to confine my remaining remarks to this.

We have agreed that globalisation involves rapidly increasing complex interrelationships worldwide. In terms of game theory, globalisation is a multi-person, non-zero-sum, time-varying game. This makes it difficult not only to handle analytically but also to simulate. Furthermore, without a clear and detailed understanding of globalisation, the task of articulating policies which African countries in general, and Tanzania in particular, should follow to maximize the benefits to be obtained from globalisation is not an easy one.

Given the complexity of the task at hand, and focusing on Tanzania, I would like to argue that the first step to be taken should be a baseline study on which aspects of globalisation are important to Tanzania, how those aspects will evolve over time and what policies, both short term and long term, Tanzania needs to adopt to integrate itself into the global economy, whilst maximizing the benefits and minimizing the costs.

A second area of concern, I would argue, is a study on the restructuring of regional groupings so as to make them and their member states participate more effectively and in a pro-active manner in the globalisation process. I am saying this is important precisely because lessons gained from general systems theory show that complex systems are best organized in a hierarchical fashion. So nation states would best participate in the globalisation process by identifying matters which should be looked at the national, regional and global levels.

Lester Thurow of MIT has argued that, whereas in the past

comparative advantage was a function of natural resource endowments and factor proportions, the key industries of the next few decades – microelectronics, telecommunications, computing (hardware and software) materials, biotechnology, robotics (including flexible machining systems) and aviation – all require brainpower. Their location will depend on who can provide the brainpower to attract them. Thus in the next few decades comparative advantage will be man-made. India, for example, has developed a software export industry worth about USD 1 billion a year in less than a decade.

The skills of the labour force are going to be the key competitive weapon in the 21st century. What education and training should Tanzania be providing to its citizens? How should it be organized? How should Tanzania prepare itself to benefit from global educational resources that are now available using modern information and communication technologies?

The society and economy that will exist in the 21st century have been loosely called 'the knowledge society' and the 'knowledge economy'. What will Africa's and Tanzania's place be in this knowledge society and how will they evolve from here to there?

The role expected of a university in a knowledge economy goes beyond its traditional roles of knowledge creation, the training of young minds, service to the community and transference of culture. The university comes to be seen as an agent of economic growth; a knowledge factory, as it were, at the heart of the knowledge economy – one in which ideas and the ability to manipulate them counts for more than the traditional factors of production. What role should the universities in Tanzania have in shaping Tanzania's position in the knowledge economy? What human capital should the universities in Tanzania develop for Tanzania to better compete in the global economy?

One cannot talk about globalisation and sustainable development without talking about environmental concerns and climate change issues. Global warming and ozone layer depletion have been addressed at the global level in the Berlin and Montreal protocols.

Although action has been taken and continues to be taken at the global level, successful resolution of environmental and climate change issues will depend ultimately on domestic policies and institutional arrangements in individual countries and the interaction of these domestic institutions with regional and global partner organisations.

The global protocols provide instruments for the global management of environmental and climate change issues, but what policies should Africa, and Tanzania in particular, adopt in order to meet their international obligations and benefit from the provisions in these protocols? Given Tanzania's development priorities, programmes and strategies, what negotiating position should Tanzania take on such controversial issues as joint implementation and trade in greenhouse gas (GHG) emissions? What implications are there for Tanzania from trade in emissions? What role should the market and WTO play in reducing GHG emissions?

We are meeting here to look at local perspectives on globalisation with the main focus being to explore research needs on globalisation. Rather than identify research needs in the economic, social, cultural and political dimensions and risk pre-empting the presentations, I have raised questions which, I hope, will serve as pointers to some of the research needs on globalisation.

It is my sincere hope that some of you will find some of my remarks of some use in your two days of deliberations on this very important topic.

Thank you very much for your attention.

GLOBALIZATION AND ITS ECONOMIC IMPACT: AN AFRICAN PERSPECTIVE

T. Ademola Oyejide

Introduction

Since around 1970, Africa's growth performance has deteriorated, both in comparison with its previous record and more significantly when placed side by side with the growth record of other developing regions of the world. There is also a general consensus that Africa's poverty situation has worsened over the same period. Attempts to understand this phenomenon have dominated economic research on Africa over the past two decades. In addition, policy responses, most notably in the form of structural adjustment programmes since the early 1980s, have concentrated on identifying and implementing policy reforms and structural changes aimed at promoting the region's economic recovery and stimulating sustainable economic development, with the main focus on poverty alleviation.

There are reasons to expect that the current wave of globalisation will have a significant impact on African economies, and there is already an active and growing debate encompassing both the research and policy communities on whether this impact is likely to be negative, positive or, perhaps, benign. This paper offers a broad and brief review of a range of issues generated by this debate and suggests a number of questions on which it would be useful to conduct further and more detailed research.

In the following section, the paper defines globalisation in terms of its economic dimension and presents a discussion of the key features of the globalisation process, as well as its implicit policy prescriptions. Next, we focus on its implications for growth, income distribution and poverty. The analysis here starts with a more general theoretical perspective and then sharpens its focus on features and considerations specific to Africa. We then address the question of whether Africa is integrated (or rapidly integrating) into the global economy and the extent to which this affects the direction and magnitude of the likely economic impact. The next section examines the extent of Africa's integration into the global economy, asks whether recent (and in many cases on-going) reforms are increasing this integration, and explores what further policy responses could be appropriate in the circumstances of different African countries. We conclude the paper with the identification and preliminary discussion of several research issues whose results might deepen our understanding of the links between globalisation, growth and poverty alleviation in Africa.

Globalisation: its meaning and key features of its economic dimension

While it is important to recognize that – as a process which involves a widening and deepening of international interactions – globalisation has various dimensions, the focus of this discussion is on the economic dimension. But even within this restricted context, globalisation can be defined both narrowly and broadly. In its narrow sense, the process of globalisation refers to the increasing flows of trade in goods and services between countries and as a share of their gross domestic products (GDP). Its broader definition extends its coverage beyond trade flows to include similar flows in the factors of production (i.e. capital and labour) and technology. As Richardson (1995) suggests, this broad definition should include the international migration of not just physical and technological capital, but also human capital (both skilled and unskilled). In other words, globalisation should mean trade booms, huge capital flows and mass migrations.

In essence, therefore, the process of globalisation can be described as the deepening and widening of cross-border flows of trade, capital, labour and technology facilitated by rapid communication mechanisms in a single, fully integrated global market. Defined in this broad way, the word evokes the image of a world in which national borders no longer matter, and in which economic agents can choose where to produce, consume, invest and save, based entirely on global considerations rather than being confined to their specific national borders.

There is indisputable evidence that the process of globalisation described above has been under way for some time. Since the 1970s, foreign trade and the international movement of capital, technology and, to some extent, labour have been extensive and increasing. Over this period, the ratio of trade to output has risen markedly virtually worldwide. Global trade has grown twelvefold in the post-war period and is projected to grow at 6% annually over the next decade or so. In the same way, foreign direct investment (FDI) has grown more rapidly than aggregate domestic investment. More specifically, FDI flows increased approximately sixfold in the 1985-95 period. While both trade and FDI flows are expanding, linkages between them also appear to be strengthening. As more and more FDI flows are geared towards serving global rather than domestic markets, they are also increasingly attracted to export-oriented economies.

The growing internationalization of various economic activities is spurred by a variety of factors, including policy decisions by many governments to liberalize and deregulate their markets and economies, as well as innovations in communications and information technology. Thus, governmental actions to substantially reduce tariffs and other barriers against the international movement of goods, services and some factors of production have fostered global economic integration by boosting trade and FDI flows. Recent advances in communication, transportation and information technologies have sharply reduced transport and communication costs and thereby significantly eroded natural barriers to the cross-border movement of both capital and technology.

The liberalization of national markets appears to be a key factor in the process of globalisation. The liberalization and deregulation movement derives its motivation from the belief that free flows of trade, and factors of production in the global context will produce the best outcome for growth and human welfare. Thus, globalisation is increasingly pressurizing governments of developing countries to further liberalize their external sector policies and regulatory regimes so as to align them with those prevailing in the more advanced and major trading countries.

In addition, the movement of capital across national frontiers, which represents the epitome of globalisation, subjects the domestic policy environment to a new discipline. This is, in effect, a loss of power for the governments of countries closely integrated into the global economy. For example, if such governments were to embark upon reckless fiscal policies, the global financial market would punish them through capital outflows. This loss of power is, however, not necessarily detrimental (Collier, 1997); what it does is essentially limit the extent to which governments can adopt extravagant policies.

It is clear that a fully integrated global economy would render national domestic policy autonomy largely irrelevant since it would limit a country's ability to confine the effects of its domestic policy within its national borders and to insulate itself against the shocks emanating form foreign policies and economic developments. In particular, a truly global economy would render futile national-level efforts to maintain economic and financial conditions at home that diverge substantially from those prevailing in the rest of the world. Hence, globalisation implies the imperative of globally harmonized policies and regulatory regimes.

In reality, however, the principles of free markets that would be an integral part of a fully integrated global economy are selectively applied. This may explain why the global market for unskilled labour is not nearly as free as that for trade in goods and services and capital. Labour market integration continues to be limited by government-imposed barriers to international migration while capital is treated as highly mobile internationally. In other words, while the current wave of globalisation has moved the world quite rapidly in the direction of an integrated global economy, it has not quite achieved the ideal of a borderless world; certain key markets remain segmented, some parts of the world remain largely isolated from the process of globalisation.

Implications for growth, income distribution and poverty

Globalisation is expected to confer certain benefits on those countries that are fully integrated into the global economy (World Bank, 1996). These benefits are derived from the exploitation of comparative advantage, better access to technology, greater ability to tap international capital markets and heightened competition. These should, in turn, improve the efficiency with which resources are allocated and thus increase an economy's potential for growth and employment creation. But globalisation is clearly not free of problems; in fact, it produces both winners and losers. It is, for instance, associated with greater instability in the world economy. It is also linked to greater vulnerability of many individual countries to external shocks which, in turn, tend to negatively affect their economic performance. As Griffin (1995) argues, globalisation is inherently associated with economic forces which tend to increase inequality in the global distribution of income. These forces operate through trade flows, capital and labour flows, as well as access to technology. For instance, gains from trade are unevenly distributed because trade liberalization has proceeded more rapidly for goods and services of interest to the industrialized countries than for those of interest to the developing countries. Similar trends towards the concentration of capital in the developed countries (where the risk-adjusted returns tend to be higher) tend to widen and perpetuate existing inequalities in productivity, incomes and welfare.

Flows of human capital as a result of globalisation are especially perverse. Skilled professionals tend to flow from developing countries to the more developed, thus worsening the global distribution of human capital. But because of discrimination in the global labour market, flows of unskilled labour from the developing countries to the developed are severely limited. Finally, the transformation of knowledge into a private commodity through the intellectual property protection agreement inhibits technology transfer to the developing countries and thus slows down the global convergence of productivity levels.

These considerations underpin the proposition that greater integration into the global economy is not only associated with benefits and costs but also that it does not necessarily offer the same potential opportunities to all countries or confront them with similar costs. This implies that in spite of the overall benefits that globalisation might bring for national (world) welfare, there are adjustment costs that are incurred by particular groups (countries) in the nation (world).

Research continues to focus on the specifics of some of the benefits and costs of globalisation using basic trade models as a convenient analytical framework. The standard Heckscher-Ohlin trade model is the favourite workhorse in this context. This model predicts that each country engaged in trade (a key component of globalisation) will export those products that use its abundant and cheap factors of production. Hence, when export booms due to trade liberalization, the demand for the country's abundant factor will increase as will the returns to that factor. The implication of this is that globalisation should favour unskilled labour in poor countries and skilled labour in the more developed countries. But widening wage inequality in both developing and developed countries as well as rising structural unemployment in the latter suggest the need for a closer examination of the factors responsible for these observed trends that have routinely been associated with the process of globalisation.

In the case of the developed countries, it is argued (Richardson, 1995, p.40) that trade opening will cause the movement of relative factor prices against pure, less-skilled labour, and in favour of skilled workers, experienced workers, and physical and technological capital with the result that wage inequality could widen. A radically different explanation is offered by Wood (1995, p.57) for the same phenomenon: his conclusion is that 'the main cause of the deteriorating situation of unskilled workers in developed countries has been expansion of trade with developing countries' because the goods imported by developed countries are more labour-intensive than those they export. Taking both developed and developing countries together, Williamson (1997, p.117) finds that 'the trend toward globalisation was accompanied by changes in the distribution of income as inequality rose in rich countries and fell in poor ones'.

Other studies (e.g. Davis, 1996 and Robbins, 1996) suggest that, even in developing countries, wage inequality typically did not fall but often rose after trade liberalization. Thus, liberalization appears to have been accompanied by greater inequality with a falling share of income for the poorest 20% in several Latin American countries. Several reasons can be offered for this result. First, manufacturing tends to be dominated by large formal sector enterprises in which wages are typically higher than in the small-scale or informal sector. Second, given the weak links between the formal and informal sectors of developing economies, globalisation tends to worsen the disadvantage of informal sector workers. Third, liberalization facilitates the inflow of capital and technology thus increasing productivity but, in the process, raising the demand for and returns to skilled labour (for which imported capital and technology are complementary inputs) rather than unskilled labour.

How would these ideas play out in the African context? Collier (1997) offers some insights with respect to this question, based on the superimposition of several Africa-specific features on the basic

Heckscher-Ohlin framework. The framework provides three mechanisms through which the broad impact of globalisation on a typical African country can be traced. The first is through trade: by producing and exporting labour-intensive products, demand for, and returns to labour are increased and hence poverty is reduced. Second, labour migration out of particular African countries is enhanced by globalisation and the African country gains through remittances. Third, the inflow of capital (which is also enhanced by globalisation) will increase productivity, improve growth, raise incomes and thus help reduce poverty.

There are several problems with this conclusion. First, it does not disaggregate labour into its skilled and unskilled components. If this is done, it seems clear that the labour category for which demand would go up as exports expand beyond primary production would be the skilled component. The same result would be obtained when the inflow of capital and technology serves as the mechanism through which the impact of globalisation is transmitted to the typical African economy. Hence, it may be expected that both of these mechanisms will produce results which widen income inequality as returns to skilled labour rise relative to those of unskilled labour; in this circumstance, relative poverty may actually rise rather than fall. A further reason why inequality might rise with globalisation is if the poor are disproportionately dependent on subsistence, while globalisation increases only market incomes.

Second, labour migration as a mechanism for reaping the benefits of globalisation is limited in view of the general discrimination it faces in the developed countries. The skilled professionals who can more easily migrate constitute a major loss of human capital to African countries – a loss which may far outweigh the remittances that they send home. In any case the most significant migration of unskilled labour occurs within Africa (e.g. from Burkina Faso to Côte d'Ivoire, and from various countries within Southern Africa to South Africa). There is a sense in which labour migration of this sort reflects the benefits of regional integration arrangements rather than those of globalisation.

To incorporate Africa-specific features explicitly into the basic Hechscher-Ohlin model, Collier allows technology (and hence productivity) to differ between countries by introducing location and transactions costs into the model. The rationale for this is that both can have across-the-board productivity effects. First, there is some evidence that landlocked countries grow significantly more slowly.

21

Second, economies that have high transaction costs (due, e.g. to high transport costs, high costs of information, difficult contract enforcement, and high cost of ancillary public services) tend to be less conducive to efficient production than elsewhere.

Countries that are subject to either or both of these disabilities tend to have a generalized disadvantage in all internationally traded activities, which is equivalent to a generalized reduction in productivity. Hence, such countries would have lower returns not only on labour, their abundant factor, but also on capital. If these countries integrate into the global economy, they are likely to experience an exodus of both factors, to the extent that these factors are mobile. Since a higher proportion of countries in African are landlocked than in other regions, and since virtually all African countries are characterized by higher transactions costs than elsewhere in the world, this model suggests that such African countries should be losing (rather than gaining) capital in the process of globalisation and should be losing labour (i.e. through the 'brain-drain'; the unskilled component of labour is prevented from migrating by foreign discriminatory practices). Evidence on the outflow of skilled professionals from Africa is provided by the 'brain-drain' phenomenon. Similar evidence regarding capital outflow comes from the data on capital flight: in the early 1990s, about 37% of Africa's wealth was held outside the region (this was as much as 70% for private wealth).

These simple models offer predictions that broadly reflect the stylized facts of many African countries. The predictions are quite bleak when taken on their face value. But a closer look indicates that policy has an important role in restoring more 'normal' results. For example, being a landlocked country may appear to be beyond a policy remedy. But this is precisely one important reason for regional integration. An effective regional economic integration arrangement could thus enable a landlocked country to escape the negative consequences of globalisation as an integral part of a larger regionally integrated market. High transaction costs constitute part of a country's policy regime and efforts to reduce the costs of transportation, information and contract enforcement will enhance productivity and thus raise the returns to its factors of production. In this sense, therefore, appropriate policies can reverse the bleak predictions described above.

Africa in the globalisation process

Whether and to what extent these issues matter for particular African countries are empirical questions whose answers depend on how closely African countries are already (or soon will be) integrated into the global economy. It is therefore useful at this point to examine the extent of Africa's participation in the process of globalisation.

Developments in the world economy have traditionally had significant impacts on the economies of African countries. World developments influence African economies through such mechanisms as changes in commodity prices, changes in the prices of African imports, flows of foreign assistance, foreign direct investment and, more recently, the external debt overhang. Recent policy reforms, including the liberalization of trade and payment regimes, were designed to propel the region into an even closer embrace with the global economy.

In spite of these changes, there appears to be no strong evidence that Africa is participating in or taking full advantage of the current wave of globalisation. Thus, African countries remain, in many respects, more weakly integrated into the world economy than other regions of the world. This summary assessment should be supported with concrete evidence. How should a country's (or region's) degree of integration into the global economy be measured? Several direct and indirect indicators are available (World Bank, 1996). The direct measures include Trade/GDP and FDI/GDP ratios; while indirect measures include creditworthiness (a measure of access to international capital markets) and share of manufactured products in exports (an imperfect measure of a country's or region's ability to produce at world standards and absorb technical knowledge).

When applied to Africa, the trade and trade ratio indicators of globalisation tell two slightly different stories. One is of Africa's marginalization in world trade, while the other suggests that Africa's trade ratio is not radically different from that of other developing regions. The first story suggests that Africa has not participated in the expansion of global trade over the past two decades and the global trend for trade to grow faster than output. There are three sets of evidence in support of this story. First, Africa's share of world exports has declined sharply over the last four decades (from 3.1% in 1955 to about 1% in 1995). Second, real exports per capita in Africa have stagnated over the last ten years or so while they have increased substantially in Asia and Latin America. Third, Africa's export product and market diversification has declined over the last three to four decades while that of other developing regions has increased. Taken together, this evidence suggests that in relation to trade, Africa has been marginalised just as the rest of the world has globalized.

The second story is based on a comparison of Trade/GDP ratios. During the first half of the 1990s, Africa's Trade/GDP ratio averaged around 41%. This lies somewhere between the 46% recorded by the East Asia and Pacific region and 38% of the Latin America and Caribbean region and is roughly double South Asia's 21%. This evidence suggests that Africa's marginalization arises not necessarily because the region is not trading enough of its output but primarily because its output and exports have not been growing. In fact, over the 1991-95 period, Africa's real GDP growth per capita was -1.5% and its export growth per capita was -1.6%. These figures compare very poorly with real GDP and export growth per capita of 8.0% and 14.1% respectively for East Asia.

Africa's experience with the world financial markets exhibits a similar marginalization trend. During the late 1970s and early 1980s, Africa received about 9% of all private capital flows to developing countries. This share fell to less than 2% during the first half of the 1990s. Compared to other developing regions, Africa does not attract significant FDI or portfolio investment flows, except for investment in the petroleum and mining sector. It therefore still relies more heavily than any other region on grants and concessional flows for its external financing needs. Thus, over the 1993-95 period, Africa's FDI flows and other private capital flows as a share of GDP averaged about 1%; Latin America's share was three times as much while that of East Asia was almost sixfold during the same period. Not only is Africa the region with the lowest FDI/GDP ratio in the world, this ratio also declined in 20 African countries during the last decade.

The two indirect measures of globalisation simply reconfirm Africa's marginal position. For instance, Africa's share of manufactures in export is, at less than 10%, the lowest in the world. On top of this, the share actually fell in about a third of African countries over the last ten years. African countries are also not regarded as being credit worthy in world financial markets. According to the *Institutional Investor* credit ratings of the mid-1990s, virtually all African countries earned the lowest (C and D) credit ratings. Since borrowing costs rise as ratings fall, their ratings indicate that most African countries are virtually locked out of private capital inflows.

This broad picture of limited integration into the global economy notwithstanding, different African countries may have to explore different routes for tapping into the globalisation process, depending on such factors as their location, their level of industrialization, their natural resource endowments and their policy regimes. Whether as a region or as individual countries, Africa cannot opt out of the globalisation process. As Kanbur (1998, p.10) notes:

> 'The central policy dilemma for African policy makers is how to take advantage of the undoubted opportunities that integration into the world economy affords for rapid growth, while managing the attendant risks for domestic income distribution in its different dimensions ...... To give up the large gains from trade, capital flows and technology acquisition is not advisable .... Thus, restricting openness to the world is not the right policy response to manage the consequences of greater openness. Rather, the right response is to have policy instruments that will balance out the various distributional changes that are bound to accompany liberalization into a globalising world.'

Some issues for research

It is one thing to conclude that African countries cannot opt out of the globalisation process but it is quite another to direct different African countries, through policy research, to the appropriate mechanisms through which they can most efficiently integrate themselves into the global economy. Collier (1997) offers a preliminary categorization of African countries based on location, natural resource endowments and policy regimes. More detailed work at the individual country level is clearly needed to validate this rough classification and derive the appropriate policy advice. A related issue – which also needs to be dealt with at individual country level – is the probable disjunction between key elements of each country's development strategy and the policy changes required to tap into globalisation. This will clearly feed into the usual debate on such questions as: How much liberalization? Which sectors should be covered? How fast should it proceed? And how should the liberalization process be sequenced and managed? Most analysts agree that globalisation has its benefits and costs; it produces both gainers and losers. Therefore, part of research priority should be an identification of gainers and losers and an analysis of the circumstances under which they gain and lose. Results of such research could assist policy makers to design incentives for firms and workers for adjusting to and reaping the benefits of globalisation.

A country's location (e.g. being landlocked) and policy regime may have important implications for the mechanisms through which it is impacted upon by the process of globalisation. It is likely that effective regional integration arrangements may ameliorate a country's locational disadvantage in the context of globalisation; while such schemes may also enhance its capacity to commit to a more growth-promoting policy regime. In both of these senses, regional integration may assist some countries to more effectively derive significant benefits from globalisation. But further research is needed to more definitively answer the questions implicit in this discussion.

The linkages between globalisation, inequality and poverty are already the subject of an emerging debate. This debate suggests that in both developed and developing countries, skilled labour reaps the gains from globalisation and that this leads to a widening of the income gap between skilled and unskilled labour and, perhaps, a worsening of relative poverty. Do the experiences of African countries confirm these trends? Apart from rising inequality with globalisation that may be due to labour market segmentation, is there any empirical support for the idea that if the poor are disproportionately dependent on subsistence, inequality will rise when globalisation increases only market incomes? A more comprehensive modelling of African labour markets which accounts for segmentation along various dimensions, including between skill-levels, rural-urban cleavages and along ethnic and gender lines should provide more robust results.

Finally, studies of the relationships between globalisation, income inequality and poverty should aim at making clearer distinctions between increased inequality and rising relative and absolute poverty. It is certainly important for the purposes of policy, to explore the questions regarding how significant poverty caused by globalisation is relative to other causes of poverty, and to which component of poverty (i.e. relative or absolute) globalisation contributes most significantly and why.

References

Burtless, G. (1995), *International Trade and the Rise in Earnings Inequality,* Journal of Economic Literature, Vol. 33, pp. 800-816.

Collier, P. (1997), *Globalisation: What Should Be the African Policy Response?* Oxford University Working Paper Series, No 97/40. Oxford.

Davis, D.R. *(1996), Trade Liberalization and Income Distribution,* Mimeo: Department of Economics, Harvard University, Cambridge.

Griffin, K. (1995), *Domestic Policies in Developing Countries and their Effects on Employment, Income Inequality and Poverty,* Background Document for the World Employment Report 1995, International Labour Organisation, Geneva.

Kanbur, R. (1998), *Income Distribution Implications of Globalisation and Liberalization in Africa,* Thematic Paper for the AERC Project on 'Africa and the World Trading Systems', AERC, Nairobi.

Oyejide, T.A. *(1998), African Trade Prospects in a Globalising Era,* Cooperation South, UNDP, New York.

Richardson, I.D. (1995), *Income Inequality and Trade: How to Think, What to Conclude,* Journal of Economic Perspectives, Vol. 9, No. 3 (1995): pp.33-56.

Robbins, D. (1996), *Trade, Trade Liberalization and Inequality in Latin America and East Asia: Synthesis of Seven Countries.* Mimeo, Harvard Institute for International Development, Cambridge.

Slaughter, M.J. and P. Swagal (1997), *Does Globalisation Lower Wages and Export Jobs?,* Economic Issues 11, IMF, Washington.

UNDP (1997), *Human Development Report 1997.* UNDP, New York.

Williamson, J.G. *Globalisation and Inequality: Past and Present,* World Bank Research Observer, Vol. 12, No. 2, pp. 117-136.

Wood, A. (1995), *How Trade Hurts Unskilled Workers,* Journal of Economic Perspectives, Vol. 9, No.3, pp. 57-80.

World Bank (1996), *Global Economic Prospects and the Developing Countries,* 1996, World Bank, Washington.

GLOBALISATION AND THE EAST AFRICAN ECONOMIES: AN OVERALL PERSPECTIVE

Brian Van Arkadie

Introduction: globalisation or marginalization?

In certain key respects, the phenomenon of 'globalisation' is not particularly new in its impact on peripheral economies. Throughout its colonial history, the Tanganyikan economy was subject to the dominant metropolitan influences of the German and then the British empires. Growth was led by production for the international market. Sisal, the largest export, had been introduced quite explicitly to meet German requirements. At Independence, the economy was heavily dependent on imports to meet its requirements for manufactured goods and even moderately sophisticated technology, and the financial sector was totally under international ownership.

Uganda and Kenya followed diverse development paths, because of the decisions made by the British colonial authorities regarding the mode of economic organisation in the 1920s (peasant export production in the former case and a settler economy in the latter). In both cases, the economies were profoundly affected by metropolitan influences. The three East African nations were already part of the global economy, through the British imperial system, at their moment of birth.

Nor was the 'transnational' corporation unknown to the colonial economy. The great colonial trading companies operated between and across continents, and had often played a crucial role in shaping political developments.[1] The impact of the global economy was a central theme in the radical literature on the East African economies.[2] Many of the issues to be confronted in relation to current day globalisation are not dissimilar to problems addressed in the past.

The specific developments in the past decades which have given rise to the hullabaloo about globalisation are:

- the increased mobility in the location of industrial production, with the resulting shift of much industrial activity from the established centres in the industrial economies;
- the greatly increased importance of international financial markets, with the resulting limitations on the capacity of national governments to pursue independent monetary and foreign exchange policies;
- the increase in the size and in the cosmopolitan character of the large corporations, rendering them less susceptible to control by their home authorities;
- with the demise of the Soviet bloc, the emergence of an unchallenged hegemony of free market economics, underwritten by a system of multilateral agreements and organisations geared to promote the operation of all aspects of international finance and trade on 'free market' principles – there is now only one game in town; and
- with the attempts to integrate the previous Soviet bloc into the international market, and the widespread adoption of liberal trade and foreign exchange policies by almost all developing economies, there is now an almost universal aspiration to participate in the global economy.

'Globalisation' has been particularly significant for the medium-sized industrial powers, who have been faced with a significant erosion of autonomy in national policy-making. This has resulted in increased pressures to conform to the free market economic models and to integrate into larger political groupings (notably the EU).[3]

The benefits which can accrue to successful participation in the global economy were particularly illustrated by the success of the East Asian economies in the long boom they experienced before the onset of the current economic crisis in mid-1997. That crisis should not be surprising[4], as the dynamic growth experienced by East Asia eventually led to over-investment and the sort of speculative bubble which has typically brought to a close periods of expansion throughout the long history of the growth of the global market. The result will be a period of depressed markets and low commodity prices. However, it can be expected that this will eventually be followed by a new upswing which will open up new development opportunities to those in a position to grasp them.

For the East African economies the longer-term question is whether the economies can be positioned to actively participate in the next boom.

For the peripheral primary commodity producing economies (that is, as they were a generation ago), the significance of globalisation during the boom years varied enormously. For the economies of South East Asia, the growth of their industrial exports and the increased mobility of capital resulted in extraordinarily high growth for a generation. Indeed, some of the concern about globalisation in Europe seems in part a nervous response to the challenges perceived as resulting from the industrialization of the Pacific rim.

For Africa, however, the story of the past generation has been quite different. Africa has experienced marginalization rather than globalisation. Even in relation to the continent's traditional role as a producer of primary commodities, the relative importance of Africa in world trade has declined. Africa has not participated significantly in the global shift in industrial production away from Europe and North America. It has not featured in the internationalization of equity markets. And compared with a number of Asian companies, its participation in the market for migrant labour has been minor.

---

[1] See John Keay (1991) for a popular account of the role of the trading company as a precursor of colonial rule.
[2] Of course, the classic works on imperialism by J.A. Hobson and M. Lenin were about 'globalization'. Immanual Wallerstein, and his associates at the Braudel Center in Binghamton, New York, has over the past two decades developed a body of work exploring the long history of the global economy. Walter Rodney's (1981), *How Europe Underdeveloped Africa,* Howard University Press, Washington DC, was surely about the global economy and Africa. Giovanni Arrighi (who taught in Dar es Salaam in the late 1960s) addressed the impact of multinationals on Africa in, Giovanni Arrighi (1967), *The Political Economy of Rhodesia,* Moulton, The Hague and, with Saul J. and Lionel C. (1972), *Socialism in Tannzania: An Interdisciplinary Reader,* East African Publishing House, Nairobi. More recently, Arrighi has addressed the broad historical perspective on globalization in, Giovanni, A. (1994), *The Long Twentieth Century,* Verso, London. Colin Leys and Michael Cowen, among others, addessed the impact of multinational business on Kenya.[3] These effects are to be seen at their clearest in the case of Sweden where, faced with the realities of globalization, over the past decade there has been a movement away from the social democratic, neutralist Swedish model, to enter the EU and to increasingly conform to the new norms of free market economy.
[4] However, this is not to imply that it was readily predictable. I edited the Asian Development Bank annual survey of the Asian Economies, Asian Development Bank, (1997) *Asian Development Outlook,* Oxford University Press, which was prepared in the first quarter of 1997. Somewhat embarrassingly, it was published just weeks before the onset of the Asian crash, but it would be difficult to expect that from its generally optimistic tone, reflecting the professional conventional wisdom of the time.

There was greater interest shown at the end of the 1960s by international business in investment in East Africa than in subsequent years. In relation to international capital movements, the only sense in which there has been increased 'globalisation' has been through the build up in dependence on foreign aid, particularly during the 1970s.

For those who are deeply suspicious of globalisation, the marginalization of Africa might be a source of congratulation, if it was the result of the success of an alternative, more self reliant strategy. However, this is very far from the case, in that the current condition has either emerged from the failure of attempts at more autonomous development (as in the case of Tanzania), or from weak performances in economies which attempted to integrate into the international economy (a possible interpretation of Kenya experience). Many African economies have been implementing structural adjustment programmes for more than a decade, which have aimed to boost foreign trade and investment. The limited success in accelerating integration in the global economy has been at variance with the hopes held out by those promoting structural adjustment.

In considering the consequences of the marginalization of Africa, a comment once made by Joan Robinson with respect to the exploitation of labour in market economies might be relevant – the only thing worse than being exploited is not to be exploited. In relation to globalisation, to be excluded from the process may be worse than being included in a disadvantaged fashion. If there is only one game in town, that is the game which has to be played.

The African continent is now of less economic interest to the rest of the world, as a market, a source of commodities, or for investment than during the colonial period. Indeed, to put it cruelly, if the continent were to disappear from the world economic scene, it would be of little consequence in the main commercial centres; this compares with East Asia – when it gets economic pneumonia, at least the northern financial markets get influenza.

Therefore the key immediate issue for economic policy research must be how to increase African participation in the global economy. Of course, a related set of questions concern strategies to maximize the benefits and minimize the costs of such participation, but there is little point in raising alarm about the dangers of globalisation when it is not even clear that African economies are participants in the globalisation process.

Colonial integration into the international economy

The options facing the East African economies in relating to the global economy may be illuminated by placing them in the historical context of the evolution of their relationship with the global economy. The impact of the colonial period on the three countries varied significantly. While the history will be well-known to those attending the workshop, it might be useful to recount the main outlines. The colonial relationship was defined by strong connections through **commodity markets** (mainly exporting agricultural commodities and importing manufactured goods), rather limited relationships through **capital markets** (there was little net import of capital and East Africa was not a major location for multinational investment, but there was a dependence on mainly British financial institutions and on Asian and British trading companies) and only a very specialized connection through **labour markets** (as an importer of professionals – and of some unskilled labour from neighbouring countries).

Uganda had been developed as a smallholder export economy, administered through indirect rule, with little alienation of African land (with the significant exceptions of the tracts of land used for Asian owned sugar plantations and for tea plantations). The successful export economy had been concentrated on smallholder production of cotton and coffee. Europeans were administrators and professionals, while trade and the lucrative production of sugar for the East African market had been in Asian hands. By striking contrast, Kenya had developed as a settler economy, with a mixed farming system producing both for export and for a protected East African market. African cash crop farming had not been encouraged, and the production of lucrative tree crops, had been actively discouraged, until the mid-1950s.[5] The effect of colonial agricultural and tax policy was to ensure a cheap labour supply for European farmers, who were also protected by prohibitions on Asians holding land in the White Highlands.

The large Asian community, excluded from agriculture, applied its

---

[5] Important change in colonial agricultural policy came with the implementation of the Swynnerton Plan, following the critique of colonial economic policy by the East African Royal Commission (1953-55)

entrepreneurial energy to commercial and (from the Second World War) industrial development.

Tanganyika, which was administered by the British as a League of Nations and then a UN Trust for four decades, operated as a mixed model of African smallholder and non-African[6] owned agriculture. Sisal, at independence the largest export, was almost entirely a plantation crop. Coffee production was roughly evenly divided between African smallholders and non-African owned farms. Cotton was a smallholder crop. Non-African farmers and plantation companies produced minor exports, such as tobacco and tea, and Africans supplied hides and skins and a number of other minor export items. At the end of the colonial period, Tanganyikan exports were roughly evenly divided between African and non-African producers.[7]

The colonial period is of more than historical interest, as the liberalization measures of recent years in some ways seek to turn the clock back to that period. And the strong presumption of current policy advice that, in the global economy, the East African economies have a comparative advantage as agricultural exporters can be assessed against that experience. What lessons about the impact of the global economy are to be learnt from the colonial economy? This is to ask a very broad question, but it is no broader that the ready assumption of a 'natural' comparative advantage in export agriculture.

One important conclusion about globalisation suggested by earlier experience is that the consequences depend not only on the nature of trade specialization, but also on the mode of organisation of production. The historical case for the positive impact of the international economy

---

[6] The non-African farming community was more diverse than in Kenya. The largest sisal producers were the Karimjees, an Asian family. The Greek community was important in tobacco and sisal, and there were many farmers of British origin – although never enough to exert the influence of the white farmers in Kenya. Germans were, of course, important in the German colonial period, but they were displaced at the end of the First World War; some returned in the 1920s and 1930s, but were again displaced by the Second World War.

[7] The structure might have been significantly different if the post-Second World War Groundnuts Scheme had not failed. This was the major economic intervention of the period of British rule. It was intended to supply the UK market with cooking oil, relieving dependence on dollar imports. It is a pity that the history of the Groundnuts Scheme has been studied very little, as the British made many of the mistakes which have been reproduced in subsequent donor initiatives.

rests largely on the performance and impact of smallholder export agriculture. Smallholder exports in a number of regions experienced periods of dynamic growth. This included the rapid expansion of cotton production in Buganda in the inter-war years, and of coffee in the 1950s and 1960s, and the extension of cotton into the East and North of Uganda over the same period, and in Tanzania the growth of coffee production in Kagera, Kilimanjaro and the Southern Highlands, and cotton to the east and south of Lake Victoria. The period 1960/62-1967 saw a sustained burst of growth in Tanzanian export crop production with lively rates of growth in the established major crops, coffee and cotton, and very high rates of what had been minor crops, such as cashews and tobacco. The fact that very high rates of growth were achieved in smallholder production of coffee and tea in Kenya in the 1960s and 1970s was therefore not so much a demonstration of a particular dynamism in Kenyan smallholder farming, as a confirmation of the negative impact of a colonial policy which had restrained African cash crop production.

The record of dynamic expansion provides good prima facie evidence of the potential of smallholder farming as a mode of insertion in the global economy. The impact on farming communities was also highly positive – funding improved housing and living standards, and education. The smallholder export farming systems supported a broad middle class of prosperous farmers, and it was from these areas that a disproportionate number of the future educated elite were recruited. This was surely a far superior way of integrating into the international economy than as wages labourers in the Kenya White Highlands or Tanganyikan sisal estates. Given the evident positive aspects of these developments in the past, what questions can be raised about this mode of development for the future? One set of issues relates to the limits of smallholder agricultural export growth. The production declines in Uganda and Tanzania in the 1970s were not evidence of any inherent limits on growth, as they resulted from policy failures. However, there are four sorts of general grounds for concern about the limits of agricultural export growth:

(a) *Geographical limits:* the areas of concentrated high income export crop farming have been geographically limited, particularly to fertile highland areas suitable for tree crop cultivation; there are large populated areas of East Africa which do not share in such opportunities, where, for example, annual export crops compete with food production in low yield rain-fed farming systems. This both limits the potential contribution to national growth (even with some sub-sectors growing at double digit percentage rates, overall agricultural growth has rarely risen above 4% p.a.) and results in the opening of regional inequality.

(b) *Limits on productivity growth:* the dynamic growth in export crops has been typically the result of the introduction of new crops of much higher market value than crops in the existing farming systems (including the displacement of existing exports crops, such as the shift from cotton to coffee in Buganda in the 1950s and 1960s) rather than resulting from physical productivity growth in existing systems. Once crops have reached their geographical limit, output growth is constrained by the possibilities of increasing yields.

(c) *Limits resulting from competition with food crops:* at the initial stages of export crop production, because of either the lack of direct competition with food production, or the economic benefits to be gained from increased specialization, export production was not tightly constrained by competition with food crops. As the East African economies have become more densely populated and urbanized, food crop production for the East African market (including cross border trade) has become an option which has increased the price supply elasticity of some export crops (e.g. competition of rice with cotton)[8].

(d) *Demand limits in international markets:* The case against specialization in primary commodity exports because of the presumed limitations of the demand side has some force at the global level, both when applied to primary commodities in general and to most individual

---

[8] Note that the literature on agricultural development in Tanzania in the 1970s and 1980s (which emphasizes poor market incentives as the reason for the decline in export production) has neglected the considerable successes in food crop production for the market. This has not only included increasing supply of traditional food staples, such as maize and bananas, but also considerable innovation, with the spread of rice, citrus, dairy, Irish potato and many other horticultural outputs. It suggests that there may now be much more of a trade-off between food products and export crops as a source of cash income than in the colonial period, which in turn is likely to either constrain the growth of export production, or mean that recovery will be partly at the cost of reductions in the supply (and increase in the cost) of food to the East African market.

36

primary commodity markets.[9] It carries less weight when applied to particular countries. The East African countries were price takers in almost all commodity markets.[10] Even in a declining market it may be possible to increase revenues by increasing market share, particularly if one is a relatively low cost producer.[11] It seems likely that higher rates of supply growth would have generated more or less commensurate increases in revenues for most crops for East African producers. Over the long haul, the problems smallholders have faced have not derived so much from conditions in international markets (i.e. negative movements in international terms of trade, although those have occurred) as from internal marketing arrangements and macroeconomic policies (particularly trade and foreign exchange policies). The vulnerability of small farmers have not been so much to the vagaries of the global economy as to the policies of colonial and national governments.[12]

The prospects for agricultural export growth have to be judged empirically, rather than on the basis of *a priori* reasoning or global analysis. Short of such an empirical study, the historical record suggests that:

⟨ with favourable incentives, producing export crops for global markets can contribute to growth in export earnings, but

⟨ such expansion may face limits which would mean that by itself it could not sustain the sort of growth in national export earnings required to underwrite sustained expansion in per capita incomes.

There is another source of concern about the impact of foreign trade,

---

[9] Prebisch, Singer *et al.*

[10] An exception might have been sisal, when Tanganyikan production was at its peak.

[11] Thus over the past decade Viet Nam has emerged as a leading coffee exporter. Deryck Belshaw always argued that it was a mistake for East Africa to participate in the International Coffee Agreement, as higher revenues could have been achieved by pursuing a strategy of increasing market share in a free market. However, it should also be recognized that if advice is being given to a number of producers then it is necessary to beware of the fallacy of composition – all suppliers cannot achieve an increase in market share, and the attempt to do so could lead to market collapse (e.g. the promotion of palm oil production).

[12] In relation to marketing boards and the promotion of monopolistic single channel marketing the continuities between colonial and post-Independence policies are striking.

related to its **distributional effects**. In relation to the colonial period, and to the current global economy, there are two apparently, but not necessarily, contradictory arguments on offer. One is the 'unequal exchange' type argument, which suggests that the nature of international trade is such as to involve the super-exploitation of Third World labour.[13] The other is the 'labour aristocracy' type argument, which suggests that the external impact is to be seen in the emergence of a privileged class supported by the external link.[14]

Plantation and settler agriculture depended on very low wage labourers, recruited from areas where there was little opportunity for cash crop agriculture.[15] Insofar as this labour was voluntary, it could be argued that it generated income opportunities above the subsistence alternative, but in practice local labour was in effect forced into wage employment by a combination of the tax system (the hut or poll tax), land scarcity (partly resulting from alienation of land to settlers) and prohibitions on African cash crop farming.[16]

Smallholder farming was altogether more benign, with Africans retaining control over land, African proprietors reaping surplus incomes in good years and a middle class of prosperous small farmers emerging. In some areas there was a sub-class of agricultural labourers[17], and where there were quasi-feudal land tenure systems, revenues from smallholder farming supported strata of chieftains.[18]

Other activities sustained by the colonial economy included the

---

[13] Emmanuel, Arrighi (1972), *Unequal Exchange: A Study of the Imperialism of Trade*, Monthly Review Press, London

[14] Giovanni A. and Saul J. (1974), *Essays on Political Economy of Africa*, East African Publishing House, Nairobi. Arrighi was strongly influenced by his initial work on the Rhodesian economy. A similar class of arguments in the Marxist literature related to the role of the 'comprador' bourgeoisie. A somewhat different argument was developed by Celso Furtado, who argued that economic inequality was required to provide a market for the sophisticated industrial products of multinationals.

[15] In the case of Tanganyikan sisal, from Malawi, Kigoma, Mozambique etc..

[16] Notably in East Africa, the recruitment of workers from Kenya's Central Province to work in the White Highlands.

[17] E.g. in both Kagera and Buganda there was widespread employment of Rwandan migrant labour. However, as this migration was voluntary, even for these low-paid workers, smallholder farming provided opportunities for improved incomes.

[18] In Uganda, the existence of quasi-feudal land tenure systems ('mailo') meant that the growth of export farming in Buganda supported an upper class of chiefs. I am not certain how far this was also true of Kagera, which shared some of the social characteristics of the Ugandan kingdoms.

traders (predominantly the Asian ethnic minority), state functions and early stage industry, discussed below.

Post-colonial strategies towards the international economy and the disasters of the 1970s

There were some similarities in the varying strategies adopted by the three East African states to deal with the colonial economic inheritance, but also striking contrasts. In the immediate post-colonial years, in all three countries the main emphases in economic policy were on rapid localization the public service and quickening the pace of social and economic development, rather than on radical economic structural change. The first round of development plans were strongly influenced by the reports of three large pre-independence World Bank missions.[19]

The strategic options facing the three economies on gaining independence were moulded by their varying colonial inheritance. Tanganyika came to independence with little industry, as part of its status as the least developed of the three countries, also evidenced by its weak transport infrastructure and its minuscule graduate elite.[20] Uganda had a much larger educated elite, better developed social and economic infrastructure and a fledgling large scale industrial sector, based on colonial State enterprise (the UDC)[21] and minority Indian capital[22]. Kenya had by far the largest industrial sector, owned by the large European and Asian[23] minority communities and by multinational firms.

Although not as large or important as in Kenya, the Asian ethnic minority communities played an important economic role in Uganda and Tanganyika, and for reasons explained below there has been a

---

[19] As Chief Planning Economist to the Government in Uganda in 1965-66 I was responsible for completing the Ugandan Second Five Year Plan (1966-71). While the Plan incorporated an effort to raise the rate of capital formation, accelerate education and achieve some diversification, the institutional framework was essentially that inherited from the colonial period, including the two important crop marketing boards, the Uganda Development Board and the Uganda Electricity Board. The two large SOEs, the UDC and the UEB, worked rather well as development institutions for many years, suggesting that in an appropriate political/administrative setting State enterprise can play a more positive role than countenanced by current orthodoxies.

[20] Comparisons need to be made with some care, for although Kenya was the most developed in terms of industrial structure and overall per capita income, the African population had the lowest per capita income and its educated elite was no more developed than the Tanzanian, until the effects of the cash educational efforts just preceding independence bore fruit (e.g. the Mboya 'air lift'). See Van Arkadie and Dharam Ghai (1969) for an analysis of the difference in the colonial inheritance.

resurgence in their importance in the 1990s – one topic in any analysis of the East African economies and globalisation has to be the location of the ethnic minorities in the larger picture.

In all three cases, the East African countries saw export diversification and structural change through industrialization as key components in the post-colonial strategy to change their relationship to the global economy. In the 1960s, industrialization was envisaged in part as an East African project, in the context of the common market.[24] All three countries hoped to gain from the common market, although it was also recognized that an active industrial policy would be required, to promote the reasonable distribution of benefits which would be required to ensure continuing political support for the common market. However, what was not recognized at that time was the degree to which the function and success of the common market was related to investment by multinationals.

---

[21] The history of Uganda colonial policy is of some interest as indicating that the adoption of State-led development policies (including marketing boards and State-owned industrialization) was far from being a post-colonial innovation. The vigorous support for State investment in industry (including the first textile mill, Nytil) under the two colonial governors, Sir John Hall and Sir Andrew Cohen, had its origins in the immediate post World War II development plan, supervised by the ecologist C. B. Worthington, which provided an interesting early environmental (neo-Malthusian) justification for industrialization, based on the view that in the long-term Ugandan agriculture could not provide sufficient employment opportunities for the growing population. An even stranger antecedent to Ugandan dirigism was provided by Winston Churchill's commentary, in Winston Churchill (1908), *My African Journey,* Hodders and Stoughton, London, where he speculated on the special suitability of Uganda as a home for State-led development.[22] Particularly the Madhvani and Mehta families, whose fortunes had been based on sugar, but also a number of medium-sized Asian-owned businesses.

[23] To protect the political powerful White farmers, Asians had been prevented from entering agriculture.

[24] In 1964 I argued that the East African market was large enough to provide the basis for successful import substitution, and that represented the most practical option for the first stages of East African industrialization. In light of subsequent orthodoxies, that view may seem both erroneous and surprising (Van Arkadie, 1964). However, at that time Latin American industrialization looked relatively successful, East Asia was not yet a home of miracles, and the first writing emphasizing the high costs of import substitution in practice were just appearing (e.g. my colleague at that time at Yale, Ron Soligo, was raising questions regarding Pakistan industrial policy). Even in retrospect, I would argue that in the common market context a couple of decades of successful industrial growth could have been achieved by concentrating on supplying the regional market, if the general economic environment had continued to be as positive as in the early 1960s.

Kenya

The radicalism of the political struggle for independence in Kenya, the underlying social pressures of landlessness and joblessness and the presence of a more explicitly leftist tendency in Kenyan political life might have suggested that it would be in Kenya that the most radical economic changes would be attempted in the aftermath of colonialism. And perhaps the most radical programme of change was implemented there, with profound changes in the rural economy resulting from the combined effects of the Swynnerton Plan, which had shifted colonial agricultural policy dramatically towards the encouragement of African cash crop agriculture, and the land settlement programmes, which had transferred a significant segment of the European mixed farms to African smallholders. However, in terms of the larger political economy, active land reform and the encouragement of small holder farming served the conservative political function of contributing to rural stability, in the context of which the Kenyan leadership pursued a policy of continuity in the industrial and commercial policy. Sessional Paper No. 10 of 1966, on African Socialism and Economic Policy, opted for the continuation of Kenya's existing relationship with the international economy.[25]

Kenya could expect to benefit from its established position as the centre of the East African common market and from its developed infrastructure (e.g. in tourism). More subtly, however, Kenyatta saw the possibility of fostering the emergence of a strong African capitalist class, so that a sub-text of the commitment to capitalism was an active policy to encourage the educated African elite to claim a stake in the ownership of the economy.[26] This model had some success for two decades, not only in generating reasonable rates of GDP growth, but also, as a result of the successful development of smallholder agriculture and rapid expansion of education, in spreading the benefits of growth.

---

[25] For a contemporary sceptical comment on the Kenyan strategy see Van Arkadie, 1970.

[26] In the land settlement programme this even went as far as an attempt to engineer a squirarchy, as a result of a specific initiative of Kenyatta, under which blocs of land (so-called Z-plots) attached to large country houses were to be allocated to members of the administrative elite. See the joint UK-Kenya Mission on Land Settlement which I led in 1966.

When Kenya began on its chosen strategy in the 1960s it was probably more or less as well developed in terms of physical infrastructure, financial and commercial institutions and the beginnings of an industrial sector as some of the economies of East Asia, which subsequently experienced spectacular export-led growth. True, Kenya has had its foreign earnings successes, in generating tourism and in diversifying agricultural exports[27], but it did not participate significantly in the classic dynamic industrial export markets, such as clothing and electronics, and in recent years its growth performance has tailed off. The reasons for the limited success of the Kenyan growth strategy should be of interest to Kenya's East African neighbours, as they shift towards more private, market-oriented development.

One factor limiting the scope of industrial expansion was the degree to which Kenya's industrialization, from its beginnings in the Second World War through the 1970s was essentially geared to supplying the protected East African market. The break-up of the East African community, foolishly applauded by members of the Kenyan political elite[28], blocked one avenue of industrial expansion. That event more or less coincided with the change of political leadership following the death of Kenyatta, breaking the link between key elements in the emerging indigenous capitalist groups and the political leadership – the effectiveness of crony capitalism may vary, depending on the cronies.

Tanzania

Tanzania presented a striking contrast to Kenya. It shifted towards a socialist development strategy, which began with the implementation of the Arusha Declaration in 1967 and accelerated in the first half of the 1970s, with the implementation of Ujamaa and of the Basic Industrial Strategy. Unlike in Kenya, the political and administrative elite were discouraged from property ownership, income policies were egalitarian and social service delivery strategy was innovative – incorporating what was in effect an early version of a 'Basic Needs' strategy.

---

[27] A part of this was 'catching up' in smallholder tree crop production (tea and coffee), which had been discouraged before Swynnerton over decades in which smallholder export crops had moved ahead in neighbouring countries. However the development of high value horticultural products was more of an innovation in the East African context.

[28] Charles Njonjo opened a bottle of champagne in the Kenya National Assembly to celebrate.

42

Even after the first oil shock, it was still possible to envisage the experiment as having the potential to succeed.[29]

However, by the early 1980s, it was evident that the experiment had failed.[30] For those for whom 'socialism' is a synonym for economic failure, the outcome requires little explanation and is therefore of little interest. For those searching for an alternative to current liberal orthodoxies, a more searching examination is required. Whatever its eventual failings, the Nyerere strategy was serious and incorporated many elements of alternative strategies still on offer. In particular, there is a need to explore whether the whole approach was flawed in principle, or whether tactical errors and avoidable failures in implementation undermined an otherwise plausible and merit-worthy strategy.

In relation to its connections with the international economy, the post-Arusha nationalizations broke off banking and other financial connections, and took much of the commercial service sector into the public sector. Initiatives both before and after Arusha displaced the Asian business community from the trading sector, which had been its mainstay. The nationalization of urban property further demoralized the Asians, who had begun to move into the industrial sector, as a result of which Asian emigration increased. At the same time, the limits placed on the development of African private business meant that in medium and large scale economic activity, foreign and minority community ownership was displaced by bureaucratic control. However, the Tanzanian technical elite was weak, and the attempt to develop the parastatal sector under a controlled and egalitarian incentive system was unrealistic.[31]

The industrialization effort (which included a pragmatic willingness to encourage foreign investment) faltered for many reasons, which have been identified in the literature. Location was haphazard, with too little coordination with infrastructural investment. After the severe

---

[29] See the sympathetic interpretation I participated in writing in 1978 (Green, Rwegasira and Van Arkadie, 1980). However, at about that time, aid agencies which had been highly supportive began to express doubts (in the case of the World Bank the big country report prepared in 1977 was a turning point). Also, at that time, critics on the left who were sympathetic to the aspirations articulated in the Arusha Declaration, had begun to mount a serious critique (see Coulson, Andew, (1974), *A Simplified Political Economy of Tanzania,* Economic Research Bureau, University of Dar es Salaam, Dar es Salaam).

[30] In 1981-82, when I worked with the Tanzanian Advisory Group, I felt that elements of the system could be retrieved (see Van Arkadie, 1983); John Loxley felt this even more strongly, as is clear from his subsequent publications about that period.

deterioration in the foreign exchange situation after 1978, new industrial capacity could not be utilized, because of the lack of foreign currency to provide inputs. Looking back on the 1970s, so many things went wrong with the industrialization effort, ranging from microeconomic factors, such as poor project design and inadequate attention to management requirements, through sectoral imbalances, which meant that many projects were frustrated by infrastructural bottlenecks, to the macroeconomic disequilibrium, which affected all economic activity, that it is difficult to establish any one clear lesson.

How far the poor export performance which contributed to the foreign exchange crisis was the result of the industrialization effort is unclear. At first sight, it might appear that the Basic Industrialization Strategy was seeking to promote industrial growth at the expense of agriculture. However, agricultural disincentives did not result from the classic mechanism of surplus transfers to finance industry – monopolistic single channel marketing transferred surpluses to a bureaucratic 'black hole' of inefficiency rather than to investment activities. Also, a large part of the industrial investment resulted in idle capacity rather than output, so that agriculturalists did not have to subsidize industry by buying expensive import substitutes.

Nevertheless, the industrial investment programme was part of the ambitious capital formation effort of the 1970s which gave rise to the macroeconomic disequilibrium, which did place a heavy burden on the agricultural export sector.

Although the main thrust of the industrialization effort was to produce import substitutes for the East African market, some explicit efforts were made to produce industrial exports. These efforts included the ill-fated World Bank financed Morogoro Shoe Factory, which deserves its place in the history of Tanzanian development failures alongside the Groundnut Scheme, somewhat more plausible Swedish

---

[31] One of the contradictions of the Nyerere experiment was that the lack of a developed African middle class meant that the implementation of radical economic policies faced little opposition, but that very weakness of the African technical and managerial cadres meant that the capability to implement a bureaucratic-led development was not there; indeed, the rapid expansion of the parastatal sector greatly weakened the capacity of already fragile government bodies. For two contemporary commentaries I made on the economic implications of the Arusha Declaration, see Van Arkadie, 1970 and 1973.

supported efforts to promote small industry export manufacture, in cooperation with Swedish firms, and investments in sisal processing. Efforts to generate industrial exports met with little success, while traditional agricultural exports declined, so that the overall result was that exports have declined as a ratio to GDP, while dependence on imports for industrial products and fuel persisted – the resulting gap being filled by aid.

Uganda

Uganda presented a third approach to restructuring the colonial economy – while aspects of developments on Uganda under Amin were farcical (when not tragic), his regime had a profound impact on the Ugandan economic structure.

During Obote 1 (that is during the 1960s), although a populist rhetoric was adopted, particularly with the 'Common Man's Charter' which picked up some of the resonance of the Arusha Declaration, the actual content of economic policy was mainly a pragmatic continuation of colonial policy. In the Ugandan case, however, the colonial regime had left in place an unusually well developed parastatal sector, with the Uganda Development Corporation already involved in industrial development and operating the largest hotel chain in East Africa, and the Uganda Electricity Board managing a power operation which supplied a significant portion of the Kenyan market.

The Amin regime had a deep impact in three ways. The expulsion of the Asians removed a group who had dominated trade and large-scale farming and were the leading private industrial entrepreneurs. Thirdly, during the Amin period and the confused years that followed his removal, links with the international economy were reduced, with the withdrawal of many foreign businesses in the face of the prevailing uncertainties, and the decline of traditional exports (particularly cotton). Also, many of the educated elite who might have aspired to careers in the professions, in the bureaucracy or in politics left the country, acquiring experience elsewhere.

With the Museveni regime, some degree of normalcy has been restored. Privatization, the restitution of Asian properties and the implementation of liberal economic policies has resulted in some economic recovery. Some of the leading Asian families have taken back their businesses. Admittedly, the plaudits Museveni has received from the donor community have to be treated with caution, both because of the poor track record of 'successes' identified by such agencies as the World Bank, and the strong prodigal son effect. Despite Museveni's very considerable achievements, exports have still not been restored to earlier peaks, the impressive record of a small group of economic policy-makers has not been matched by improvement in the capacity of government ministries, which remains very weak, peace is fragile and the political succession unsure.

As recovery takes hold in the Ugandan economy, long-standing problems of Uganda development will have to be confronted. Uganda is even more dependent on coffee earnings than in the 1960s. The landlocked position of the country significantly influences comparative advantage, making the country dependent on the transport infrastructure of Kenya and Tanzania, and suggesting that comparative advantage might lie in production of food and industrial goods for the East African market.

However, Uganda also has some potential advantages. As a result of her early lead in education (which was sustained throughout the confusions of Amin and after) and the experiences of the refugee elite, Uganda probably has more entrepreneurial capacity than Tanzania. The fertility, compact size and relatively well developed infrastructure gives Uganda an edge. However, it remains unclear what position Uganda can aspire to in the future international division of labour.

Structural adjustment and afterwards

After a decade of structural adjustment, some economic successes have been achieved. Both Tanzania and Uganda have succeeded in restoring a degree of macroeconomic stability and dismantled much of the dysfunctional system of government economic control. The economies have benefited, with a revival in economic activity. Entrepreneurs have responded to the opportunities provided by policy reform, with higher levels of output and private investment.[32] Perhaps the most fundamental development to be observed throughout East Africa has been the emergence of a large class of successful African small businessmen, in transport, trade, construction and services, which may provide the pool of entrepreneurial talent required for longer-term success.

However, while there has been a revival in export activity, this has not carried exports above levels achieved in the early 1970s, failing to reach levels projected in structural adjustment programmes and leaving the economies excessively aid dependent. One big question for the coming decade is whether persistence with liberalization policies will eventually yield benefits in terms of much more rapid exports earnings – whether the East African economies will effectively join the global economic game.

As of this moment, the global economic environment is not very propitious. The indications when this paper was drafted were that having led the upward swing in the last boom, the East Asian economies were leading the global economy into a depression, triggered by the bursting of a speculative financial bubble. Nevertheless, in the cycles of market activity an upswing can be expected to follow that crisis, and in that upswing, new opportunities for accelerated growth will emerge. What will be required to take advantage of such opportunities?

Any attempt at detailed scenario formulation would be foolish, in that it is a characteristic of entrepreneurial opportunities that they are unpredictable and the development successes of one generation are not reproduced in the next. That having been said, it may be useful examining what is the potential which East Africa has to take to the international marketplace.

Potential comparative advantage

The East African market, if the common market re-emerges as a working reality, is sufficiently large to provide a base for some industrial growth, particularly for those products where transport costs and other factors provide natural protection. However, experience of the 1970s (particularly that of Tanzania) demonstrated that the growth of the domestic market and the possibility of local industries supplying that market are constrained by foreign exchange availability, which ultimately means foreign exchange earnings (as aid is unlikely to be a growth industry over the long term).

---

[32] For a review of the Tanzanian experience of structural adjustment see Van Arkadie, 1996.

The possible sources of foreign exchange earnings (i.e. of effective participation in the global economy) can be considered under four main heads: traditional exports, tourism, mining and industrial export processing. The possibility of generating significant foreign exchange from labour remittances (as a number of Asian and Latin American did in the past) does not, at this point, seem great.

Factors likely to condition the prospects for traditional exports are similar to those discussed above in the consideration of the colonial exporting economy.

Tourism is already established as a leading sector in Kenya, and is now fast growing in Tanzania. Uganda, lacking a coast, does not have the same prospects. The development of the industry in Tanzania requires a more integrated approach than has so far been in evidence (e.g. it is not clear that such matters as policies towards aircraft landing rights[33], visa fees, land allocation, etc. are subject to any sensible economic analysis in relation to their impact on tourist revenues). Also, there is a need to promote greater national participation (to increase the domestic value added). In particular, there is a need for study of mechanism, whereby small and medium scale African businesses could increase their participation in the servicing the tourist trade.

The *mining* potential of East Africa has hardly been developed. Issues which will require continuing attention are numerous issues of public policy in relation to both the artisanal[34] and the large scale sector. The licensing and taxation of mining and negotiation with multinationals is a highly complex area, in relation to which East African experience is limited. It should also be noted that in the not unlikely event of substantial mineral earnings being generated in the future, the management of the disruptive macroeconomic effects would require careful attention (the differing historical experiences of Nigeria, Zambia provide ample examples of potential problems and policy response).

---

[33] Limitations on traffics rights on intra-East African movements seem largely to be motivated by the wish to protect the national carrier, in effect offering an implicit subsidy, irrespective of whether this is a cost-efficient method of subsidy. It might well be in Tanzania's larger economic interest to encourage the use of the considerable excess capacity of international airlines on these routes to increase passenger traffic. Needless to say, this would also be to the benefit of long-sufering East African travellers. Subsidies are best transparent, so that government and the public can be aware of the cost.

Industrial export processing has been an important component of most of the successes of export-led growth of developing economies. To date, this has not developed to any significant extent in East Africa, and in the current global context, prospects may not seem too good, given the number of new entrants (e.g. among the 'follower' economies of East Asia, such as Vietnam and Bangladesh) and the prospect of heightened competition from established producers (such as Thailand and Indonesia, who have severely devalued their currencies). Yet there will be fast growth on a global scale in such activity in the future, and its location is neither predetermined or very predictable.[35] It may be worth exploring ways in which the considerable entrepreneurial capacity demonstrated by African small business in supplying domestic markets could be tapped to supply export markets (e.g. a concerted effort to develop sub-contracting).

Lessons from East Asia and the role of government

While there is a lively debate about aspects of the East Asian successes (e.g. about the role of the State), there are some necessary conditions suggested by the successes of East Asia prior to the current crisis. There are four conditions which to varying degrees the East Asian successes shared:

a) they enjoyed high rates of technical progress and growth in agriculture (where applicable – i.e. not including the City States);

b) they all promoted exports vigorously, whether in the context of an open economy (e.g. Hong Kong) or along with strong protection in the domestic market (e.g. South Korea);

c) the region achieved high savings rates to varying degrees (although one factor contributing to the crisis was high levels of borrowing by some of the countries);

---

[34] In Tanzania, there has been an explosive growth in artisanal mining of gold and gemstones. The almost weekly record of serious accidents suggests the need for greater supervision, while experience elsewhere in Africa suggests that the taxation of artisanal mining presents great difficulties (see the study of taxation of artisanal mining in Sierra Leone by S. Kamara and myself (1991).

[35] In this regard, I remember participating in a seminar in the mid-1960s on Mauritius, whose economic future seemed totally bleak. While I remember suggesting that the island should concentrate on acquiring a comparative advantage in labour-intensive industrial export, that was no more than an off-hand seminar comment, and at that time the subsequent success of Mauritius as an industrial exporter seemed a totally remote prospect.

d)   the governments in the region were effective in maintaining macroeconomic balance and in ensuring the provision and maintenance of basic infrastructure.

Such conditions are not yet present in East Africa. Smallholder agriculture, as discussed above, has experienced dynamic growth in the past, but the prospects for sustained growth remain problematic. None of the countries has a coherent and vigorous programme of export promotion in place. A degree of macroeconomic balance has been achieved, but at the cost of restricting government expenditures below levels needed to maintain government capacity and basic infrastructure is inadequate and poorly maintained. For example, the recent experience of Dar Es Salaam has included a succession of crises – power, water and transport. When competing in the domestic market, such constraints are irritating but not fatal, as they are shared by competitors. When competing internationally, random water and power supplies and hopeless transport infrastructure can be fatal impediments in competition with better organized economies.

Reversing the current weaknesses would require a focused government programme, based on clear priorities and pursued with determination bordering on the ruthless. Nothing in the current behaviour of governments suggests that this is a likely outcome.

Over the past three decades, during which many connections with the global economy weakened, aid dependency increased, particularly in Tanzania[36]. Increasing aid dependency was evidence of poor performance in competing in global markets which increased the relative importance of aid flows, but has also been a significant, if not major, contributory factor in the weak competitive position of the East African economies. Aid has never performed particularly effectively as a growth input, but there are three particular reasons why it may not contribute to success in the global economy.

(a) *The decreasing growth component of aid programmes.* Over the past three decades there has been a substantial shift in the emphasis of aid programmes away from support for economic growth towards a range of charitable and other paternalistic objectives. Aid has become increasingly concerned with the promotion of an agenda which finds favour amongst the pro-aid lobbies in the donor countries – concerns for democracy/poverty/gender/environment, rather than economic growth as such. Significantly, the high growth economies of East Asia have been quite effective in resisting pressures from such lobbies. [37]

(b) *The erosion of national capabilities*. Aid dependence has contributed to the erosion of the capability of national governments to take effective initiatives. The 'development programme' is largely made up of donor financed and designed projects, and policy initiatives originate with the donor agencies.

(c) *The distortion of incentives*. It has been argued that in the case of Tanzania, in the early 1980s, aid had a sort of indirect 'Dutch disease' effect, underwriting a distorted policy regime (e.g. allowing the authorities to postpone exchange rate adjustment). Since that time, there may have been a more direct negative impact of aid on exchange rate levels. Apart from such possible macroeconomic effects, aid has had strong effects on the incentive system, particularly for the educated elite. Be it acquiring a grant, launching an 'NGO' to attract donor support, acquiring jobs in donor funded project units, or simply attending courses, workshops and seminars, aid has become an important source of income for the educated elite, particularly in light of the decline in real incomes from government and parastatal employment. The relatively soft market for services by donors may direct energies away from the riskier and more difficult challenges of entrepreneurship in the commercial economy.

The role of Asian business

The liberalization and privatization of the East African economies under structural adjustment has not yet resulted in the significant entry of the great multinational companies. While no systematic study is available on new patterns of ownership, the impression gained from casual observation is that the main effect has been a resurgence of the Asian business community, not only in areas where they traditionally played a dominant role, such as trade, but in new areas such as banking and finance, and real estate development.

---

[36] Given the popularity with donors of the current regime in Uganda, a similar effect is likely there.

[37] See the introduction and my paper with Harris Mule in Havnevik and Van Arkadie (1996)

The resilience and persistence of Asian business in the face of expropriation, expulsion and restrictions on trade is quite remarkable. The presence of this active business community could be a source of strength, as well as a potential political irritant, for the future of all three East African economies. During the 1970s, with the Diaspora of the Ugandan Asians, and the less dramatic migration of Asians from Tanzania and Kenya, East African Asians established themselves in the UK and North America, and many business families now have connections there as well as in the Indian sub-continent.

In many East Asian economies, the Overseas Chinese communities have played a strategic entrepreneurial role in their dynamic structural change. Could the Asian business community play a similar role in East Africa?

One impediment is the widespread resentment of the Asians, which made their expulsion from Uganda a popular political move, and renders their position politically fragile. However, in East Asia the Overseas Chinese have been the subject of resentment and there have been incidents of extreme violence.[38]

Given the strategic importance of the Asian business community in the East African economies, it has been the subject of surprisingly little formal study.[39] Any research programme seeking to explore East Africa's future role in the global economy should include research on Asian business.

New foreign actors in the economy

Another aspect of change in East Africa, which is also observable in West Africa, is the active role of new entrants from other parts of the Third World. Particularly noticeable has been the engagement of South African firms following the end of apartheid. In such areas as mining, brewing, and service activities (including hotels) South African large businesses have become important players, and many small-scale entrepreneurs are also seeking opportunities. There have also been interest shown by East Asian investors, including Malaysian involvement in banking and finance and communications, Thai involvement in gemstones, Chinese in construction, etc. Again, while these tendencies are clear from casual observation, they have yet to be subjected to serious study.

A national business class?

A further question which may be posed relates to the impact of a strategy of integrating into the global economy on the internal distribution of economy and access to economic opportunities. In particular, what are the prospects for the emergence of a national business class? There are a number of reasons why this is important. As Albert Hirschman once put it, whatever the relative merits of a nation specializing in primary commodity trade, there can be little advantage in specializing in supplying labour, leaving the supply of capital, and all that goes with it, to foreigners. There is also a political economy issue related to the development of a national business. It is not so much a matter of the old Marxist debate about the importance of having a 'national' rather than a 'comprador' bourgeoisie, as the negative consequences of having a political and administrative elite without a stake in, or strong connections with the economic elite. Without some connection, the government is unlikely to be responsive to the needs of business, business will be susceptible to populist attack, and State functionaries can see business as essentially a source of rents.

Under structural adjustment, those in formal employment have not done well, and the technical and administrative elite have, with some exceptions, fared particularly badly. This is not surprising, as in Tanzania the edifice which has been dismantled was in many ways geared to the needs of the bureaucratic elite (although as the system went into crisis, real incomes began to erode – although even then, the system of allocation of scarce commodities favoured those in office. By comparison, a group of small-scale business people, in such activities as trade, transport, mining and construction has emerged which do well in the market economy. Even in the professions there has been a burst of entrepreneurial activity, as health care and education are increasingly provided on a private basis[41]. On the other hand, with the demise of the parastatals in Tanzania in seems likely that for some time African leadership role in the large business sector will be minor. In Uganda and Kenya there are larger groups of African big businessmen.

---

[38] Ghai Yash and Ghai Dharam (eds) (1970), *Portrait of Minority Asian in East Africa,* Oxford University Press, Nairobi
[39] Ghai Yash and Ghai Dharam (1965), Asian in East Africa: Problems and Prospects, *Journal of Modern African Studies,* 3(1):35

How can the emergence of African big businessmen be encouraged? This is a difficult and controversial area. In Asia the basic approach to the promotion of indigenous big business has been through one variation or another of 'crony capitalism', that is the political regime favouring selected business groups – this may be through explicit policies (Malaysian preferences for the Bumiputra under the NEP), or through informal networks. In the current crisis, crony capitalist has been receiving much criticism, and in the extreme cases of the Philippines under Marcos or the latter part of the Suharto regime in Indonesia such stigma seem well justified.

Similarly, the crony capitalism of the former Soviet Union does not seem to be working well.[42]

Nevertheless, successful participation in international capitalism (which is what globalisation is about) is probably more likely with a developed group of national capitalists, and in the history of capitalist development this has typically involved an intimate relationship between the State and business. The trick is for the State to promote big business to the benefit of the national economy, rather than the Swiss banking system.

An agenda for study

This paper has provided a discursive *tour d'horizon*, which has touched base with a wide range of historical and contemporary issues. There are a number of areas of possible detailed study implicit in the discussion, some pointed out in passing. There are two general conclusions which deserve emphasis. The first is that the requirements for successful engagement in the global economy should be explored on the basis of a concrete understanding of the evolving East African social reality. This probably requires rather more emphasis on the study of the sources of wealth and the organisation, connections and strategies of powerful economic groups, as compared to studies of poverty, which currently receive the lion's share of attention.

---

[41] In Uganda and Kenya, private provision of education is a long-standing practice, but it was largely banned in Tanzania in the Nyerere period. Now considerably more children enter private high schools than public institutions, and the mushroom growth of private hospitals and dispensaries has come to the point at which two private colleges now offer medical training in Dar es Salaam.

The second point is that successful participation in the global economy requires some understanding of its working and of the successes and failures of strategies adopted by other nations. In this regard, research by Tanzanians has been far too parochial, a bias supported by overseas centres of funding and graduate study which tend to feel that Tanzania is always the most appropriate topic of study for Tanzanians.

---

[42] For a discussion of the difficulties of creating a capitalist class *de novo* see Van Arkadie and Karlsson (1992).

LOCAL PERSPECTIVES ON GLOBALISATION: THE ECONOMIC DOMAIN

S.M. Wangwe and F.M. Musonda

Introduction

Globalisation is defined as the rapidly increasing complex interactions between societies, cultures, institutions and individuals worldwide. It involves a compression of time and space and is a process which 'stretches' social relations, removing relationships from local contexts to 'distanciated' global ones. Rapid advances in technology, growth of world trade and competition, and policy changes towards economic liberalization are among the major catalysts of this process. Specifically globalisation has been reflected in trade and financial liberalization, the internationalization of production, distribution and marketing, freer flows of factors of production and the globalisation of competition.

As an economic phenomenon, globalisation is usually taken to mean the increasing density of economic integration among countries, reflected in an increasing share of output employed in a country belonging to and being managed by nationals of other countries and increased financial integration between countries. Globalisation is facilitated and stimulated by a lowering of impediments to cross-border activity through technological progress, e.g. in transportation and communications and/or through a lowering of policy or political barriers, e.g. tariffs, investment restrictions, conflicting national standards or regulations on the environment, labour etc.

Due to globalisation, some countries are emerging as winners while others are relegated to the position of losers. Winners tend to be those countries which interpret the signals from the changing world economy correctly and make the necessary adjustments to cope with the new world economic conditions. Changes in East Asia in the 1970s and 1980s and more recently in some Latin American countries in the 1980s and 1990s have shown that countries can make a turnaround and improve their position in the world economy. The era of globalisation has coincided with the revolution in information technology (IT), which has sharply reduced the cost of international information flow; this has facilitated trade and capital flows by reducing the cost of communications.

Globalisation as a worldwide trend or process has been made possible by fundamental revolutions in technology, transportation and communication, and led by the big transnational corporations and banks. The process of globalisation is driven by ever-increasing global trade and financial services, primarily conducted by the headquarters of transnational corporations in global cities. It can therefore be concluded that globalisation is driven by the actions of individual actors, firms, banks and people, usually in the pursuit of profit, and often spurred by the pressure of competition. It is thus best understood as a phenomenon that reduces the economic 'distance' between countries and continents.

The main objective of this paper is to contribute to the discussion of local perspectives of globalisation by focusing on the economic domain. It is accepted that national economies are affected by global flows – human, financial, cultural, technological and communications. This paper describes the process of globalisation and analyzes the economic effects of this process in countries such as Tanzania. The first introductory section deals with the definition and the extent of globalisation. Section two discusses the process of globalisation. Section three examines its implications at the local level. Section four looks at regionalism and globalisation and section five presents a number of appropriate steps for developing countries to take to make the jump from the national economy to the global economy. The final section contains the conclusions and suggestions for further areas of research.

The process of globalisation

The process of globalisation is said to have gathered momentum during the 1980s, following the gradual rejection of trade restrictions nurtured by the strategy of Import-Substituting Industrialization (ISI) adopted by the majority of less developed countries (LDCs) in the post world War II period, and the dissolution of the socialist system which had insulated its members from the world economy (and indeed from each other). Others mention the large-scale reforms introduced in China.

Global trends show that the pace of global economic integration has accelerated over the past decade. During the 1980s the pattern of internationalization and globalisation was further facilitated by deregulation and the globalisation of finance, and by the enabling features and pressure from new technologies. New forms of inter-firm agreements developed into major instruments for international technology transfer. These tendencies threaten to marginalise many developing countries from globalised information networks and may invoke the role of the state in setting rules and a code of behaviour for firms engaged in global competition. Globalisation is characterized by a new ranking of the factors creating interdependencies whereby direct foreign investment (DFI) in manufacturing and services rather than trade is leading internationalization and is influencing locational and trade patterns.

The pattern of capital flows and the role of firms have also changed. The number of Transnational Corporations (TNCs) has increased and the number of home bases has also increased. One consequence of this increase has been the increasing role of TNCs in exporting capital in the form of FDI. Further evidence from this area suggests that alliances are prevalent in global oligopolies, serving as vehicles for the transfer of technology between firms, achieving economies of scale, building technical standards and accessing markets, skills and resources.

Elements of globalisation

Flow of goods and services

Increased flows of goods and services between nations due to a reduction in protection of all forms: quantitative trade restrictions (tariff and non-tariff barriers). It is to be noted, however, that there has not been a corresponding increase in the mobility of labour, especially of the unskilled variety, which the LDCs are relatively abundantly endowed with.

Share of imports and exports

The share of imports and exports in overall output provides a ready measure of the extent of the globalisation of goods markets. As a result of the easing of tariffs and quotas, more efficient communications and falling transportation costs, trade has increased for many developed countries. Their exposure to international trade picked up again in the late 1980s, coinciding with their movement towards trade liberalization. While there has been a rise in the ratio of exports to total output, this understates the degree of product market globalisation, as more and more output in the advanced economies consists of largely non-tradable services: education, government, finance, insurance, real estate, and wholesale and retail trade.

Rapid development of financial markets

The financial markets have developed rapidly, and there has been an increase in the international mobility of capital, due to the lowering of obstacles to its movement. The daily volume of capital flows throughout the world stands at about USD 1 trillion (May 1998). Most of these flows are not transfers of savings surpluses to regions where savings are in short supply, as in the past (World War I), but consist mainly of speculative capital that investors may withdraw at any time if they feel it to be necessary. Technological advance has also given rise to very sophisticated forms of financial transactions, investment and derivatives, which makes it impossible to meet the conditions of transparency and complete information to participants needed for the markets to function.

Technologies

Another element of globalisation consists of the flow of technology. Although increased trade and capital flows have by and large meant an increased flow of technology between nations, not all aspects of globalisation have had an unambiguously favourable effect on it. The information and knowledge sector in particular have benefited from new technologies, but the impact of new information and communication technologies is not only confined to these sectors. ICT has become a widespread mass technology with a much wider scope of influence, affecting virtually all sectors of society.

The implication of this is the end of geography as a defining factor, characterised by globalisation of the capital and financial markets, goods markets, specific labour markets and information and knowledge markets. Potentials for the worldwide linking of different processes in the production chain are expanding and there is an opening up of market opportunities in several areas.

Implications of globalisation at the local level

In the following section we discuss globalisation in its local perspective. We have mentioned that globalisation is driven by goods and services (trade), technology and capital. Below we try to explain how the effects of globalisation are translated locally.

Globalisation is a powerful force and its impact will vary for different nations. This is particularly true for a country like Tanzania, one of the least developed countries in the world. The characteristics of LDC economies put them in a weak position as far as globalisation is concerned. These characteristics include low levels of export diversification, technological underdevelopment leading to inflexibility in adapting to changing market forces, low telephone density, underdeveloped infrastructure, underdeveloped financial markets and instruments, lack of adequate institutions, and incoherent laws and regulations to attract the inflow of capital. As a result of these factors, LDCs benefit less from globalisation and are even marginalised. In addition, there are a number of unique factors inherent in the process of globalisation that impact on local people. Some of these issues are discussed below, with a specific focus on developing countries.

Possible effects of globalisation and the position of LDCs

Globalisation can be beneficial and welfare enhancing, but it can also have negative effects. It is said to aggravate or reinforce income and technological gaps between nations, especially between those which are sufficiently prepared or endowed to take advantage of globalisation and those which are not. Certain social groups may be excluded from the benefits of IT because of insufficient exposure to learning and the acquisition of knowledge and to the new skills that IT-based processes require. Globalisation may widen the 'knowledge gap' between the skilled and less skilled members of society, leading to inequalities in wages and income. Small enterprises, unable to invest in new technologies, may be squeezed out by competition, and globalisation widens the gaps between the modern and non-modern (informal) sectors. In general we can conclude that globalisation and integration may have different implications for countries like Tanzania.

Trade, investment and competition

A number issues are of concern to developing countries like Tanzania in international trade, especially with the increase in globalisation. These include the volume of trade, the degree of diversification, access to developed markets and the terms of trade.

Globalisation and Multilateral Trading Arrangements

The intensity of globalisation has necessitated an increased use of multilateral trading arrangements. The trade agreements in the GATT Uruguay Round are one of the new instruments available to regulate this process of integration. The agreements created the World Trade Organisation (WTO) to supervise the results of the Round and to continue negotiations on trade-related issues. Many other Rounds have been negotiated to try and regulate the process of globalisation in trade, investment and other areas and ensure that most countries come out as winners.

However, for many developing countries, including Tanzania, market access barriers are still abundant, especially to developed countries. These include traditional tariff and non-tariff border barriers, with which much of the pre-Uruguay Round trading system was concerned. In addition, in today's world of far-reaching integration, there are other barriers, including investment conditions, domestic regulatory conduct (including standards-related issues, the licensing of services or service providers and merger procedures), structural differences in the functioning of markets and anti-competitive practices.

Preferential access

As a result of multilateral negotiations, the preferential trading arrangements which African countries had acquired through the GATT or through the Lomé Convention with the European Union are under attack. It appears that the Uruguay Round will dilute many of the discriminatory aspects of regional agreements, for example by reducing tariff preferences for regional partners through multilateral tariff reductions. Although the Uruguay Round Agreements made allowances for many of the least developed countries in Africa, the signals are clear that the future of preferential trading arrangements is bleak. This will have repercussions for developing countries like Tanzania, and in most cases they will be negative. The reduction of Most Favoured Nations (MFN) tariffs will erode the margin of preferences that many African countries enjoy. The Uruguay Round, as it relates to Africa, has also been criticized for resulting in improved but limited market access, higher food prices for net food importers and other issues which African countries are resisting because they feel they will have adverse effects.

62

The favourable access that Tanzania is now enjoying but not as yet utilizing to the full is likely to last only to the extent that it does not threaten EU industries. There are already indications that some of these preferential provisions have been weakened in the recent Uruguay Round negotiations. Second, the favourable position of countries like Tanzania in terms of access to the EU market partly derives from restrictions on Asian exporters under the Multifibre Agreement (MFA). This may induce Asian producers to relocate to countries like Tanzania, as suggested by South East Asian investments in some countries in Africa (e.g. Mauritius, Nigeria). Rules of origin, however, are likely to limit this trend if it expands enough to threaten EU industries. Third, although this is often denied, there are indications that the former socialist countries of Eastern Europe will most likely compete with countries like Tanzania in the European arena of trade relations and other economic cooperation arrangements.

The Uruguay Round is associated with possible constraints on development policy resulting from Trade Related Intellectual Property Rights (TRIPS) and Trade Related Investment Measures (TRIMS). In the context of TRIPS, the Uruguay Round has enhanced the process of appropriation and formalized the process of universalisation of IPR standards of protection.

There is a tendency for countries in the North to form larger trading groups. This may guarantee the members access to larger markets, but will likely restrict the access of many poor non-members to industrial country markets.

Discriminatory policies

European Union trade policies essentially discriminate against imports from the developing countries. Even under the Generalized System of Preferences (GSP) and the Lomé Convention arrangements, the assistance offered is subject to unilateral termination by the European Union (EU) on grounds of 'graduation'. The EU advocates selectivity in the application of safeguards (i.e. temporary import barriers imposed in order to protect domestic industries at risk) and is demanding the protection of intellectual property owned by nationals or companies of its member states in the developing countries. The question of access is particularly important for exports of manufactures. The recent intensification of protectionism in the North has subjected developing

63

countries' manufactured exports to discriminatory restrictions precisely in those areas where the have a comparative advantage.

A number of internal factors also affect exports from developing countries such as Tanzania to developed countries. These include trade regulations, economic policies, political factors, market size, pattern and growth, competition, and price structures. These internal factors limit the extent to which these countries can participate fully in a globalized world trade system, even where potential benefits exist.

Domestic policies

Domestic regulations are primarily responsible for the reduced volume of exports from individual countries. Economic and political factors have more of an impact on macro policy. Protection policies, tariffs and non-tariff barriers applied by the exporting countries have a negative effect on exports by fostering inefficiency and reducing price competitiveness. Internal taxes are an important determinant of the competitiveness of local exporters and limit the exportability of products to developed countries. Protectionism in many developing countries has, however, been considerably reduced.

Product requirements

Here there are a number of issues or factors which are likely to hinder the market accessibility of exports from developing countries. These include the nature of the product itself (technical specifications, design and styling, size, colour, materials, method of use etc.), packaging requirements, transport methods, protective requirements, handling methods, conditions for storage, and identification and information requirements (e.g. labelling, language, legal requirements). Some exporters from developing countries lack knowledge of these requirements and at times fail to comply with them.

Marketing practices

Obstacles to market access for exporters from developing countries that fall under this category includes transport, sales and distribution channels, pricing strategy factors, services expected by buyers, advertising and sales promotion. Significant factors in the area of transport, for example, include freight rates, speed and frequency, reliability, risks and packing requirements. In many cases internal transport systems are in bad shape, and in some areas, products fail to move even within the same country.

Price structure

This is important in three areas: the price to end-users, trade mark-ups and ex-factory prices. There are also practical limitations, including the supply of competing products and the prices of competing products from developed countries. Sometimes competing products from developed countries are of a high quality, but can be marketed at a low price due to the cost advantage enjoyed by their producers.

Changing market conditions

Most exporters in developing countries are currently faced with a number of obstacles arising from changing market conditions, including an increasing need to respond react rapidly to changes, fiercer competition and growing customer demand in globalized markets, and an interest in outsourcing certain aspects of production, distribution, sales service support functions. Overall, the trend suggests that changing market conditions now require firms to meet more refined and personalised customer tastes, as well as society's collective needs. Markets are becoming more segmented, with quality and timely delivery becoming important factors in competitiveness. Global production networks are developing (for example, in sports shoes). Developing countries may only be able to enter such markets by tying themselves to major names and meeting their production requirements. Unfortunately this has proved to be a difficult strategy to realise. Consequently the market accessibility of exports from these countries remain slim.

For developing countries, especially LDCs, another factor is a lack of adequate investment capital to invest in new technologies and spend on R&D to develop/improve export products to meet the requirements of markets in the developed countries. Foreign capital inflow has not been very forthcoming for a number of reasons, including an inadequately conducive investment climate. A further factor is lack of access to or utilisation of modern technology, such as information technology to link markets.

The transition from a command to a market-oriented economy has caused specific problems in many developing countries. These include a lack of institutions, legislation and regulations (such as competition law, product and consumer standards) to support investment and inform exporters. In some countries, the private sector is also insufficiently developed, flexible and dynamic to engage in modern production and export or to meet the challenges of new and demanding markets.

Investment

Foreign direct investment (FDI) by transnational corporations (TNCs) now plays a major role in linking many national economies and building an integrated international production system (the productive core of globalisation of the world economy). TNCs deploy their tangible and intangible assets (capital, research and development capacity and technology, organisational and managerial practices, trade links) with a view to increasing their competitiveness and profitability. At the same time, the deployment of these assets by firms strengthens the resource base of countries and their capacity to produce, to reach and expand markets for their products and to restructure their economies – in brief, to improve their overall economic performance.

Despite efforts made in Tanzania to improve the existing investment regimes, the flow of investment has been marginal, especially from outside. The FDI boom in developing countries has largely bypassed Tanzania and other countries in Africa. Sub-Saharan Africa (SSA) received FDI flows worth USD 1.8 billion in 1994 (the equivalent of the flows to New Zealand), while North Africa received USD 1.3 billion. Most FDI in Africa continues to be concentrated in a small number of countries endowed with natural resources, especially oil. Africa's share of developing countries' investment flows declined from 11% in 1986-90 to 6% in 1991-93 and to 4% in 1994 (World Development Report, 1995). The International Finance Corporation (IFC) has established several programmes in recent years (e.g. the African Project Development Facility, the African Enterprise Facility). However, the IFC's investments in Africa have averaged only USD 600,000 compared to an average of USD 12.3 million elsewhere in 1994. By 1994 the share of SSA in IFC investments was about half the level of the 1970s and 1980s (Helleiner, 1996). Net resource flows to Africa, which primarily consist of official development finance, saw a sharp reduction from USD 24.1 billion in 1992 to USD 19 billion in 1993 – a fall of nearly 21%. This was largely accounted for by a decline in bilateral development finance. As the decline in official development finance was not compensated for by either increases in private capital flows or increases in export revenues, the decline, in effect, contributed to the reduction in imports. Therefore, countries like Tanzania are being bypassed by investment flows and technology, and the market access advantages that are usually associated with such investment flows.

Some factors that explain the low investment flows to developing countries

Low investment flow to Tanzania can be explained by domestic and external factors. It is generally proposed that the success of a country in attracting foreign direct investment depends on the investment climate which the country offers. Enabling macroeconomic indicators and a favourable regulatory framework help determine the investment flow to that country. But this is not universally accepted. Over time, the causes of investment flows to a country have been a central debate, because they also provide valuable clues as to sustainability of the flows. Researchers divide the causes into two main groups: external or 'push' factors (i.e. basically foreign interest rate trends) and domestic or 'pull' factors (mainly economic policy improvements). There are, however, other subjective sentiment-based factors in international markets such as the 'herd response', subjective and transitory 'pull' factors relating to recipient economies, including temporary interest rate surges after financial liberalization, and export-price booms and other 'spillover' effects from large to small countries.

Collier (1995) explains that Africa is currently marginalised because of four main factors. These include insufficient reforms, insufficient scale and low-level traps, the high-risk environment and weak restraints. The thesis of insufficient reforms argues that though reforms to date may have substantially narrowed the gap in economic incentives between Africa and other locations, they have not eliminated it. Location decisions continue to reflect the presence of this gap, which has been partly caused by continuing policy discrepancies, such as higher rates of corporate taxation, and partly by the legacy of previous policy disparities such as the neglect of infrastructure for the productive, as opposed to the social, sector. The thesis of insufficient scale and low-level traps argues that Africa has an inheritance of relatively small markets and small-scale production, as well as lower stocks of human capital, and consequently, relatively few examples which others can copy. It has missed an opportunity for manufactured export growth, and is now facing a growing cost disadvantage in comparison with other rapidly growing regions, such as Asia. Although Africa has cheaper labour, this provides little leverage in view of the small share of labour costs, especially so long as the policy and infrastructure environment, although no longer overtly hostile to private manufacturing exports, remains inferior to that of Asia.

In addition to the problems posed by insufficient scale and low-level traps, a major obstacle to successful take-off is the perception that Africa's investment climate is more risky than that in Asia. Africa is subject to the risks and shocks of policy change. These risks discourage irreversible investments, so agents postpone them in favour of liquidity, even if they are not risk-averse. Collier explains the weak restraints in Africa in terms of the weakening of the 'agency of restraint', which serves to enable an agent to bind himself to a particular course of action. Weak agencies of restraint contribute both directly and indirectly to marginalization. Indirectly, they account for the high-risk environment: the weakness of the army means that governments, and hence policies, can change without notice; the weakness of the central bank means that macroeconomic policy can change abruptly; the weakness of audits means that taxes can change abruptly. Domestic sources of finance for investment are limited, and foreign financing is deterred by the lack of exit routes.

Competition

Under globalisation, international competition is less between nations and more between firms. Firms in individual countries, including developing ones, now must compete more fiercely than in the past for a share of the expanding world market in goods and services. This is because many more countries have abandoned the inward-looking strategy of the past and there is hence more openness. The fierce competition for a share of the world market has challenged individual firms to increase their levels of competitiveness. While a large number of firms participating in the global market is supposed to create more competition, the competitiveness of individual firms will depend greatly on factors internal to the firms and at country level. As border barriers have declined, private barriers to competition have grown more significant. More and more international trade disputes involve private business practices that allegedly block the market access of rival firms. Globally there is a closer link between trade and investment policies and hence competition, and yet competition is far from perfect.

The *business environment* in which economic units must be prepared to operate is characterized by unprecedented opportunities to tap new markets, while traditional markets are changing dramatically towards competitiveness. Competition is increasing not only between traditional adversaries in traditional markets, but also from new entrants and from the disintegration of barriers to previously protected markets. With competition arising from diverse and unexpected sources, enterprises can no longer be confident about their market shares; they must constantly be prepared to face stiff competition. Overall, the trend suggests that changing market conditions now require firms to meet customer tastes that are more refined and personalized. Society's collective needs, as expressed through a wide range of democratic and associative mechanisms, are becoming more segmented, with quality and timely delivery becoming important factors in competitiveness. Global production networks are developing. This calls for new forms of interaction between producers and customers. Such interaction with more demanding and better informed customers is an essential factor for growth and competitiveness.

Many developing countries, including Tanzania, have not created a conducive environment for firms to compete in the global market. The weakness of many developing countries in this area has resulted in a lack of competitiveness of their firms, leading to divestitures, privatization and even closure of firms that cannot compete. Closures mean a loss of employment opportunities, which has not been fully compensated by jobs created as a result of increased trade.

New technologies and the implications of changing technological conditions

Technological change has important implications for the competitiveness of all economic activities in an economy. The policy implications of changing technological conditions are likely to surface at two levels: a focus on monitoring new and emerging technologies with a view to making policy decisions relating to adopting and learning about the new technologies at the right time; and a focus on the internal conditions of technological characteristics and demand.

Recent technological developments have led to shifts in the composition of factors of production, with a considerable decline in raw materials, energy and labour inputs and an increase in knowledge intensity. Material-saving innovations have led to a decline in the consumption of natural materials and their replacement by new and advanced ones, which are of better quality, stronger, flexible and light.

The implication for Tanzania is that decisions about which export products should be given priority will need to be made with due consideration of developments in technology and conditions in the world market. Technological developments have influenced the pattern of manufacturing industry in the highly industrialized countries considerably as services take the lead, with new skill and capital-intensive services (such as information science) gaining ground. This makes elasticities more difficult to predict and the growth of many traditional capital goods industries (e.g. construction materials, electrical machinery industries, general engineering, machine tools, iron and steel industries) has slowed down.

Changing industry boundaries

Technological change has resulted in redefinition of industry boundaries. Where key factors of success can be shared, the limits between businesses (industries) tend to be blurred (e.g. computers, telecommunications and office automation). Where technological change leads to a reduction in the sharing of costs of key resources the result may be de-segmentation of the industry into smaller units. The distinction between the manufacturing and service sectors is increasingly blurred by their interconnectedness. The competitiveness of manufacturing firms now depends crucially on the quality of interactions with the services sector, notably business services (which collect, treat and supply specialized information) and key infrastructural services.

Changing structure of employment and skill requirements

The structure of employment is changing with a shift from manual to mental labour as indirect production/support work is gaining ground over direct work. Practical skills have to be complemented by higher levels of theoretical skills in science and modern technologies and there is preference for personnel with multidisciplinary skills. As a starting point, user-oriented strategies towards new technologies can result in improvements. The relevant question is how much learning is necessary for the effective use of new technologies. Computer literacy and basic electronic hardware maintenance skills are likely to be essential.

Information Technology

The global spread of the information revolution has moved slowly in Tanzania as in many African countries. For example, full access to the Internet is still limited and many parts remain without any electronic connectivity at all. Overall, investments in technology in the form of

70

R&D is very low and has been declining. In 1970, Africa spent only 0.33% of its GDP on technological investment. This fell to 0.29% in 1990, a very low level compared to other countries, where the percentage is larger and growing.

In addition, the infrastructure that access to IT requires – especially education and computer literacy – may accentuate differential access based on various factors such as income. The social groups that are largely excluded from literacy and numeracy are likely to face exclusion in the use of IT. Access to IT for social groups which are economically disadvantaged is also limited by the affordability of hardware. In addition, information available on the electronic super highway itself has some characteristics which are inherently exclusionist, in the way the content is culturally determined (symbols, images, sounds and the language). These and other characteristics residing outside the hardware technology are important in influencing access to IT. Many developing countries like Tanzania are not well integrated in information technology and in some important technologies they are excluded.

Globalisation, liberalisation and fiscal squeeze

Efficiency objectives, as well as multilateral commitments, have led many developing countries to reduce trade taxes, in particular those on imports. Scaling down protectionism was part of broader structural adjustment measures aimed at encouraging the competitiveness of individual economies and at reducing rent-seeking behaviour. Foreign trade taxes, however, have always been a large and potential revenue-raising device for developing countries, accounting for up to a third of tax revenue. For Tanzania, in the 1996/97 financial year, import and excise duties accounted for 35% of total tax revenue. This high dependency on trade taxes is attributed to the fact that they are easier to implement, and do not require complex administrative systems. Ending protectionism in its traditional form has, therefore, resulted in costs in terms of foregone revenue, which must be budgeted for even if the supposed resulting increase in growth makes up for part of the losses in the long term. In Tanzania and many other countries, there has been a kind of 'double jeopardy', with trade taxes being reduced in the quest for increased openness, but with growth not managing to compensate for this decrease in the tax base.

Financial liberalisation and globalisation

One of the assumptions made when liberalizing the financial markets in many developing countries was that this would attract foreign capital inflow for investment purposes. As indicated above, for many countries in Africa this has not been the case and foreign investment is still quite low. But for those countries where foreign capital investment has increased, its growing importance has at times created a serious risk of cyclical disturbances to the development process. In a period of expansion when prospects seem healthy, capital inflows can accelerate beyond the absorptive potential of some countries. It can then become tempting for governments and private firms to borrow on the international credit markets. This can read to serious over investment, with a large deficit on the current account of the balance of payments.

As the productive and banking sectors of the economy are being increasingly privatized, the roles of governments are being redefined; they become guarantors, rather than hands-on economic agents. However, in an increasingly volatile world, this role is becoming more and more burdensome. Worldwide, the incidence of banking crises has increased in recent years. In this context, governments are increasingly called upon to rescue banks, and expensive bail-out packages often have to substitute for the strict enforcement of prudential regulation.

Bailing out the banking sector is looked at as a primacy because of the domino effect that a bankruptcy might produce. This includes the effects on small depositors and creditors, the impact of a liquidity squeeze on the manufacturing sector, and the potential loss of confidence of foreign investors, which may ripple out to other sectors of the economy.

Two aspects of liberalization have been cited as contributing to banking crises in developing countries: inadequate preparation for financial liberalization (in terms of strengthening banking standards and supervision) and the effects of large-scale capital inflows in creating a lending spree during the upswing of the business cycle. Apart from the consequences for public budgets, financial crises and currency volatility raise distributional issues.

Environmental degradation and globalisation

Trade liberalization connected with Structural Adjustment Programmes and globalisation has meant increased imports of many products, as well as the dumping of sub-standard products. These products, and/or their packaging, may be environmentally unfriendly. Trade liberalization has also implied increased export activities, increasing pressure on land, soil degradation, unsuitable mining activities, too much mining with inadequate technologies, over-logging threatening forestry products. All of these activities have dire consequences for the environment and contribute to unsustainable development.

As indicated above, globalisation has implied increases in international trade which challenge individual countries to increase their levels of competitiveness. The need for competitiveness to access markets can place pressure on the environment, as a result of the over-utilisation of natural resources, the use of inferior production techniques to minimize costs, and of techniques that are not very environmentally friendly.

Regionalism, globalisation and the local perspective

Regionalism and globalisation are compatible. The principle of subsidiarity, or optimal decentralisation, can be usefully applied within an overall global framework of rules and regulations. Regional arrangements can be seen as a necessary complements to, and essential building blocks for, a system of global governance. Regionalism as a form of international governance is related to the changing position of the state. It is no longer possible to regulate purely on the basis of national jurisdiction. The alternative of multilateral rule-making is also difficult, especially when one is considering national interest groups. Regional integration can offer a middle way that preserves the notion that citizens and their nations are still in control of events. This makes deeper integration possible in certain regions to cover competition policy, investment and even the free movement of persons. Integration in world markets through regionalism can thus be phased according to the differing economic circumstances of the countries concerned.

Other political motives for regional integration include, for example,

73

increasing the countervailing power of smaller states in multilateral economic negotiations. Regional security also plays a role. Regionalism can be used as means of achieving integration at a higher level. It should not create an inward-looking community that excludes new members and seeks to protect itself by erecting tariff barriers, but should be open. Regionalism is not an alternative to globalisation, but can be a complement, helping developing countries to achieve a phased integration into the global economy, while preserving their own identity. For regionalization to function in this manner it should not be imposed from outside but initiated by the countries themselves.

Appropriate steps for developing countries to make the jump from the national to the global economy

Globalisation as described above is a process which is difficult to avoid, and in one way or another countries find themselves drawn into the process. Since it cannot be avoided, it is imperative for developing countries like Tanzania to make every effort to participate in the process in a beneficial manner or at least minimize the risk of losses. One important step is to increase the negotiating capacities of developing countries in the regional and global arena, so that they can make their needs and wants clear. There is also a need to incorporate all the stakeholders (civil society, private sector, etc.) in regional and international negotiations.

National policy-making

National policy-making mechanisms and processes need to be designed so as to take into account regional and global implications. In this regard, there is a need to establish a consistent mechanism for discussing the implications of various regional and global issues for national level policies and vice versa at national level or with interested parties.

Regional and global macroeconomic policy coordination and programming will need to be adopted in order to minimize inter-state economic distortions and harmonize various national policies. To achieve regional and global market integration in a gradual and phased manner an institutional missing link needs to be put in place in the developing countries.

This missing link is a regional and global forum for economic policy analysis on issues which need to be addressed by member governments now in order to move closer towards economic integration in the longer term. Such a mechanism should have the capacity to analyze the fiscal, monetary and financial systems, the exchange rate and trade issues which affect the region, and should provide the venue for the regular ministerial and technocratic dialogues necessary for the achievement of progressive convergence on macroeconomic parameters. The capacity to undertake such policy analysis needs to be created and incorporated within the regional institutional framework.

At the sectoral level, there is a need to evaluate the capacity and actual performance of existing regional institutions and address the question of their utilisation and coordination with national level institutions more critically. These institutions need to be used more effectively.

In a number of sectors, the ability to remove constraints and fulfil the investment requirements (including access to new technology) necessary to raise the level of competitiveness may require a regional rather than a national solution. For each of these sectors it is recommended that efforts be made to identify cases where a regional solution is better than a national solution. These regional solutions should be articulated and ways of integrating them into national policy making should be identified.

The role of the state

The quality of policies is critical to the speed of integration, globalisation and growth by, for example, ensuring macroeconomic stability, adopting realistic exchange rates and making adequate investments in infrastructure (especially telecommunications).

The dangers of marginalisation can be reduced and the benefits of globalisation enhanced through policy moves aimed at, for example, shaping new trade relations, exploring ways of improving market access, improving access to new technology, building technological and organisational capabilities for enhancing application and adaptation of new technology, and improving other infrastructural conditions for application of IT. Technological development requires effort.

Much of this effort is expected to take the form of tangible and intangible investments. The former is the traditional material and physical assets, while intangible investments refer to human and financial resources that are allocated to R&D expenditures and other forms of spending on technology, training, business services, marketing and the acquisition and exploration of software.

In recent years there has been a tendency to pursue a 'hands-off' attitude towards the role of the state, especially in Tanzania. Yet governments elsewhere are playing a leading role in shaping new trade relations and promoting advances in technology. In addition to the crucial role that governments are playing in forging new trade blocs (e.g. the North American Free Trade Area (NAFTA), the EU), their role has been instrumental in helping firms to acquire international competitiveness.

Building on strategic trade theory and administrative theories of the firm, as well as the conventional explanations that focus on country characteristics, it has now become clear that when industries become globally concentrated, visible hands (of TNCs and governments), rather than the invisible hands of the market, emerge to guide trade.

It may be useful to emphasize that while Tanzania must avoid the mistakes of the past, efforts to influence Tanzania's position in the new global trade relations will require an active role by government. The role of the state will need to be reinvigorated to provide a strategic lead in facilitating the grasping the opportunities which the new world economy may have to offer, especially on the technology front. It will also be necessary to enhance the role of the private sector and civil society in that direction.

The case for selectively supporting specific high-potential industries through government policy has been demonstrated to varying degrees in the experiences of the developed countries and the NICs. In addition, export performance was the main practical measure of progress towards international competitiveness but detailed strategy in this highly uncertain area led to reformulation in the light of information acquired during implementation (market signals, perceptions about industrial operations and potentials).

Trends in automation have shown that state intervention is necessary in various ways: the development of education and skills; providing consultancy assistance; awareness activities (including applications and demonstration projects); enabling infrastructure and information channels for technology transfer from publicly supported technology institutes and decentralized applications centres; enhancing technology supply (upstream) by supporting domestic technology suppliers and improving access to foreign suppliers; product development support; helping with organisational changes; process development and process applications support modernizing industries which have failed to adopt best practice technologies (e.g. by providing finance to beat their investment barriers); support programmes for diffusing new technologies; and market identification, exploration and development.

There will continue to be new challenges in the area of policy formulation, taking into account the increasing overlap of previously distinct areas of policy-making, such as industry, telecommunications and IT and the institutions involved in this process. Two policy issues are relevant: support for industry in its efforts to develop technology, markets and competitiveness; and establishing and maintaining the legitimate regulatory functions of government.

Market orientation and private sector development

This approach relies more on market incentives and automatism than on administrative discretion for its incentives and preferences. One implication is that public intervention should focus on policy formulation and a role which creates a global and regional policy environment that will enable market-based integration to work. The private sector should also be made more accessible than in the past.

In order to promote the role of the private sector in global and regional economic cooperation and regional and international trade it is important that business associations establish modalities of cooperation, create strategic alliances and exchange information.

Implications of WTO

The implications of the Uruguay Round negotiations and agreements for the region should be addressed. The extent to which anticipated difficulties in market access can be mitigated through intra-regional trade should be explored. The implications of new issues (i.e. trade in services, TRIPS, TRIMS) should be explored, particularly for the role of regional integration. One possible implication is that the case of regional cooperation in the production and delivery of services, joint investments and collaboration in technology transfer and technology adaptation efforts may be stronger with a view to enhancing competitiveness in the respective areas. It should also be recognized that many of the discriminatory aspects of regional agreements may be diluted under the WTO. Regional integration arrangements will be more open and outward looking.

One important policy implication of various trade cost reductions would be to encourage investment activity in the SSA region. Regional cooperation should, therefore, recognise investment promotion as a major concern. Trade should be accompanied by investment flows, which should be encouraged by the creation of guarantee mechanisms for cross-border investments. Appropriate investment mechanisms should be put in place, incorporating some elements of a 'regional policy' which would be designed to influence, through incentives, the allocation and location of investment even at the cost of some loss of the full benefits of integration.

Many studies have also shown that firms in developing countries have adapted with respect to the characteristics of raw materials (type, quality and input-mix), down-scaling, product quality and product mix, simplicity, and capacity and factor intensity. These firms tend to produce simpler lower technology, low-cost products which require little marketing ability to sell on the world markets, have a higher propensity to form joint ventures with other local firms, have used more local human resources and raw materials, and have often down-scaled imported technologies. The case study of the Indian joint venture in Thailand showed that firms from developing countries, being themselves at the learning stage, transfer not only the know-how but also the know-why (UNESCAP, 1990).

However, various obstacles inhibit further South-South technological cooperation: lack of information, inadequate institutional framework and economic and legal barriers. There is a need for a shift in trade policy in the direction of an improved South-South trading infrastructure, liberalization of intra-South trade restrictions, forging organisational ties to enhance the exploitation of economies of specialisation, and creating an effective and innovative capacity for more efficient appropriate processes and products.

Promotion of South-South inter-firm linkages and cooperation arrangements should be viewed as complementary to the kinds of benefits which can be obtained from inter-firm networks and cooperation arrangements with TNCs from the North, and not necessarily as substitutes. The Abuja declaration on the establishment of the African Economic Community is an encouraging step. Its implementation, however, should involve taking first steps towards establishing the institutional framework to spearhead the development of these kinds of inter-firm linkages and cooperation arrangements not only within Africa but between Africa and other regions.

If the potential benefits from Trade Negotiations Committees are to be realized, domestic policies on the development of the technological capabilities of domestic firms, education and vocational training, investment, trade, technology adaptation and R&D can play a crucial role. However, in the context of the emerging world market and new technologies, the question of forging new forms of networking with TNCs and identifying the conditions under which the role of TNCs could be complementary and supportive of efforts by developing countries like Tanzania towards the enhancement of international competitiveness remains important and deserves special attention. The leading question here should be in what ways Tanzanian firms can forge inter-firm linkages and cooperation arrangements which are conducive to the development of technological and other capabilities that are necessary for making gains in international competitiveness.

The liberalization of trade in products where intra-industry trade is high can have far-reaching allocation efficiency effects as market fragmentation (characterised by too little competition and too many small firms unable to benefit from the economies of scale) is reduced. This is achieved by reducing the costs of entering a particular market and the real cost of trade (by removing various forms of red tape). In the case of regional integration in Africa, not only would larger regional markets replace small national markets but supplies from a neighbouring country could also easily satisfy even geographically isolated markets within the country. In this sense, market fragmentation can be reduced if regional markets preclude the setting up of very small plants in some corner of the country.

In many respects the conventional advantage of low labour cost *per se* is being undermined by the increasing importance of competitive characteristics other than cost of production, notably, product/service quality and just-in-time delivery. To cope with these requirements will require a greater effort to develop design, marketing and new organisational and linkage capabilities in addition to selectively acquire new technologies.

These market and technological changes are likely to have considerable implications for the shift in production towards knowledge intensity and requirements for the kinds of capabilities that must be developed to cope with the changing situation. First, greater effort will be needed to monitor these changes with a view to adapting to the new situation. This will often imply selective adoption of new technologies in production and marketing at the right time and in the right applications, according to the dictates of quality, precision, and speed and productivity requirements. Second, a greater effort will be needed to create a conducive environment for the development of core capabilities within firms and in the institutions that interact with those firms to cope with the changing conditions. The role of the state will need to be reinvigorated to provide a strategic lead in facilitating the tapping of opportunities which may arise from the new world economy.

Conclusion and further areas of research

The purpose of this paper was to describe and analyze globalisation and its local perspectives. Globalisation was defined as the complex interactions between societies, cultures, institutions and individuals worldwide. We have shown that changes in the world market and in technological conditions in the world economy in the recent past, in particular in the last decade, affect all countries including developing countries like Tanzania. The developments pose new challenges to developing countries; they have to maximize the benefits and minimize the costs of globalisation.

We have discussed the areas of intense globalisation in trade, which pose a challenge to developing countries in terms of market access. We have indicated that much of the flow of investment has bypassed many developing countries. The paper has also indicated that the intense competition due to globalisation is causing problems for developing countries because their firms are unable to withstand the hyper competition. Developing countries also lag behind in technology (including information technology), which is having a marginalizing effect.

The development of open competition, accelerated by trade liberalization initiatives, has shown that even to sustain regional markets, competition with other regions of the world will have to be faced sooner or later. There is always a danger of losing the regional markets to competitors from other regions. Even if imported products are not as suitable to local conditions, competitors from outside the region have sometimes penetrated regional markets by supplying their products at lower prices or of a better quality. Thus specific local and regional markets can be lost to others if continuous efforts are not made to develop competitiveness in terms of quality and price.

Globalisation as described above is a process which is difficult to avoid, and in one way or another countries find themselves drawn into the process. Since it cannot be avoided, it is imperative for developing countries like Tanzania to make every effort to participate in the process in a beneficial manner or at least minimize the risk of losses. One important step is to increase the negotiating capacities of developing countries in the regional and global arena, so that they can make their needs and wants clear. There is also a need to incorporate all the stakeholders (civil society, private sector, etc.) in regional and international negotiations.

National policy-making mechanisms and processes need to be designed so as to take into account regional and global implications. In this regard, there is a need to establish a consistent mechanism for discussing the implications of various regional and global issues for national level policies and vice versa at national level or with interested parties.

Regional and global macroeconomic policy coordination and programming will need to be adopted in order to minimize inter-state economic distortions and harmonize various national policies. To achieve regional and global market integration in a gradual and phased manner an institutional missing link needs to be put in place in the developing countries.

This missing link is a regional and global forum for economic policy analysis on issues which need to be addressed by member governments now in order to move closer towards economic integration in the longer term. Such a mechanism should have the capacity to analyse the fiscal, monetary and financial systems, the exchange rate and trade issues which affect the region, and should provide the venue for the regular ministerial and technocratic dialogues necessary for the achievement of progressive convergence on macroeconomic parameters. The capacity to undertake such policy analysis needs to be created and incorporated within the regional institutional framework.

At the sectoral level, there is a need to evaluate the capacity and actual performance of existing regional institutions and address the question of their utilisation and coordination with national level institutions more critically. These institutions need to be used more effectively.

Further areas for research
A number of issues raised in this paper call for further research:

〈   Identification of forms of local organisations/institutional frameworks which will mitigate against the negative effects of globalisation. The main thrust could be analysis of the possible roles and prerequisites for non-governmental organisations, community based organisations, trade unions, business associations, private organisations and the like.

〈   Investigation of the significance, mode and role of national policies in the globalisation process.

〈   Determination of how the local institutional framework can be integrated into international institutional structures for effective globalisation.

References

African Development Report, African Development Bank, ADB, Abijan, 1995.

African Review, Department of Political Science, Dar es Salaam, November, 1996.

Bhalla, Ajit. Globalisation, *Information Highway and Marginalisation*, IDRC Concept Paper, 1996.

Collier, P. The Marginalisation of Africa. *International Labour Review*, Vol. 134 (1995): pp. 4-5.

Drew, E.P. and F.G Foster. *Information Technology in Selected Countries.*

The United Nations University, 1994.

ECA Framework to Build Africa's Information and Communication Infrastructure (April, 1996). This is an internal document presented at the EAC's 22nd conference of ministers responsible for Economic and Social Development and Planning in Addis Ababa, Ethiopia, 30th April - 3rd May 1996.

Helleiner, G. K. (1996), *Linking Africa with the World: A survey of options*, Draft, AERC.

Lall, S. *et al.* (1994), *Technology and Enterprise Development in Ghana under Structural Adjustment*, MacMillan, London.

Ministry of Foreign Affairs (1998), *The Implications of Regionalism and Globalisation for Developing Countries*, The Hague.

Moshi H.P.B. (1996), *Public Enterprise Reform and Privatization in Sub-Saharan Africa*, Final Report Submitted to CODESRIA, Dakar on 'African Perspective on Structural Adjustment Programmes in Africa'.

Mulira N.K (1995), "Managing Information Technology in Uganda: Strategies and Policy Formulation". *Information Technology and Development*, 6:95-105.

Sodersten, B. (1980), *International Economics*, 2nd edition Macmillan.

South Commission (1990), *The Challenge to the South*, The Report of the South Commission, Oxford University Press, Oxford.

Streeten, P. (1996), *Costs and Benefits of Globalisation*, Draft for IDRC.

Tanaskovic I.W., J. Tocatlian, and K.H. Roberts (1994), *Expanding Access to Science and Technology: The Role of Information Technologies*, UNI.

LOCAL PERSPECTIVES ON GLOBALISATION: THE GOVERNANCE DOMAIN

Jenerali T.K. Ulimwengu

Introduction

As we prepare to enter the 21st century and a new millennium, a number of issues are being debated with increasing intensity. One such issue is globalisation. Although not a novel idea, it has nevertheless assumed a new currency, which cannot be disassociated from recent events in certain regions of the world.

Apprehension abounds and clarification is being sought about phenomena which are at once exciting and frightening and about which very few seem to be able to state many things with a high degree of certainty. Whether it be the negative effects of capital inflows and outflows that caused the recent Asian financial crisis, renewed awareness concerning international terror systems, or the scare of the so-called millennium bug, there is uncertainty abroad and this has, quite naturally, spawned a healthy if sometimes confused debate. People, nations, communities and institutions want to know so that they can plan their activities and face the dawning millennium with greater confidence. Tanzanians too try to make sense of what is taking place in the world, which will surely affect them and is to some extent already affecting them.

At this juncture there can be no ready answers for most of the questions posed, because the effects of the current acceleration of certain processes have not been fully felt or comprehended.

Globalising or globalized?

One of the questions most frequently asked in the course of this debate is whether we, as a poor, backward and underdeveloped African country have any reason to celebrate the advent of globalisation, whether there is anything in it for us. This is a legitimate question, given our long and painful history, which shows us that every time we have come into closer contact with the more developed world, and thereby engaged in unequal exchange, we have come out the losers. We thus have the right to ask ourselves whether all this is not a new-fangled euphemism for the firming up of our ties to imperialism and neo-colonialism. For, apart from the levels of intensity and the vertiginous technological implements in use, globalisation is not a new phenomenon to Africa and the Third World generally. It is only in the process of rearming, with a view to making deeper and more effective penetration into, and control over the peoples and resources of the world.

Nobody should ever make us forget that we were globalized from the moment we made contact with traders from the outside world, whether they came looking for ivory or slaves. But probably the first formal act of concerted globalisation was the Berlin Conference of 1884-85 and the partitioning of Africa. Since then the African continent has remained globalized. For a long time our rulers came from London (and Paris and Lisbon). Our governance was experimented on in Nigeria. Our laws came to us through India. Our production was organized for British factories. Our markets were for their finished goods....

Even with the end of colonialism our countries continued as appendages of the economies of the metropoles and the developed world generally. In addition our behaviour, economic activity and governance had to be conditioned by the 'Cold War' and the geostrategic requirements of Washington and Moscow and their respective allies.

The end of the Cold War ushered in a new era of 'democratisation', plural politics, multi-partyism and 'good governance', all of them handed down to us, like Tablets from the Mount, from Washington. And all the time our economic policies, plans and programmes have been closely directed by the World Bank and the International Monetary Fund, both of which will do Washington's bidding.

These historical and contemporary realities must combine to alert us concerning anything that looks like an attempt to push us further into an arrangement that we have already found disadvantageous to us. This is why I believe it is legitimate for people to be sceptical about the effects of greater globalisation and whether we are destined to play any active role. The issue is whether the whole world, us included, is globalising or whether part of the world will be the globalizers while the rest of the world produces only globalizees.

Facing the inevitable

Having stated the foregoing one must hasten to add that there is no way any country or community can insulate itself from the effects of this so-called world order, disorderly as it is bound to be in cases. It is also true that the weaker members of the international community are in no position to significantly influence the course of events. In fact even certain sections of the North, in a number of aspects, may be forced to accept realities they would not have consciously wished.

But it is also true that, depending on our willingness and ability to read the situation correctly and organize ourselves properly, there might be advantages. Whatever the case we must brace ourselves and rise to the challenge. If globalisation means, *inter alia*, the intensification of the circulation of capital, finances, goods, services and ideas with little regard for traditional national boundaries, we must work toward making at least part of that capital, those finances, goods, services and ideas come from us, that we participate proactively in the process of globalisation.

What kind of governance?

One of the major institutions that have come under increasing scrutiny in the debate on globalisation is the state, its nature, size and role in a world that is supposedly breaking down national frontiers and moving toward supraterritoriality. This is a crucial matter for every nation in the world, precisely because the state has traditionally been looked upon to perform certain tasks, to provide certain public goods, that are considered vital to the survival and orderly development of any society. Any development that modifies the nature of the state, however mildly, must of necessity have ramifications in all the socioeconomic fabric, affecting governance and spawning new power relationships.

Supraterritoriality and the disappearing state

But is it true that the state is disappearing, that we are entering an era of borderlessness and statelessness? The intensification of commercial and cultural exchanges through means that are not controlled or directed by any state may seem to suggest this state of affairs. Today so many decisions are made in corporate board rooms and affecting the lives of millions of people who do not even know the existence of these transnational companies. These decisions are too often made without regard for any state, although their consequences may cause chaos and even lead to the overthrow of a dozen states at a go.

What happened recently in South East Asia is an illustration of this phenomenon. Even if it is possible to say that the affected countries were mismanaging their own economies, still the immediate cause of the collapse was decisions made by a handful of investors. We know the turmoil that this crisis caused and continues to cause to this day, both in that region and elsewhere, leading to bankruptcies, loss of savings and jobs, instability, and riots, rendering whole nations ungovernable. What happened to Indonesia, and is now happening to Russia, has its reasons that may have little or nothing to do with the Indonesian or Russian government. Free flow of capital, made possible by instant communication, dictates what market to buy into and buy out of at the speed of the click of a mouse.

It is true that this new and frightening reality has rendered the state less influential than it used to be in the traditional setting. Transnational corporations and sovereign individuals act in complete independence of governments and states and are not accountable to anyone.

And yet it may not be correct to suppose that the state is disappearing. It is certainly under attack and it may have to adapt and modify itself in order to meet the new challenges, but it is doubtful whether we are witnessing its imminent demise.

Backlash

There may even be a backlash. Peoples and nations may begin to feel that accelerated globalisation is causing them too much misery and that they need to return to the era of state control and regulation for security. We are therefore likely to see the return of currency and price controls and greater intervention by the state in economic and financial management. In some cases this has started happening. What is taking place in Russia today, reversing the trend of almost ten years, is illustrative of this point. There is a real danger of the situation getting completely out of control and making way for the rise of an ultra-nationalist government to take over power. Malaysia is another example where the Prime Minister has fallen out with his finance minister and heir apparent over differences in appreciating the causes of, and the cure for the current crisis. More and more nations, finding themselves in an impossible economic situation, created by a rudderless and inhuman globalisation, are likely to seek the comfort and protection of the national government, even resorting to tariff and non-tariff barriers to trade.

It is all very well to talk of a world economy, which is supposed to bring improved welfare for the peoples of the world. But when that order brings suffering, frustration and disillusionment to the extent that we have witnessed in South East Asia, which nation is likely to believe that that system is in its interest? Clearly, globalisation is in the interest of the economically stronger members of the international community, and the disparities between these and the weaker members, countries of the Third World, are not showing signs of abating. On the contrary they are deepening. The recently established World Trade Organisation has all but ignored the interest of the Third World in favour of the North. When one hears the countries of the North harping on about democratisation, plural politics, good governance, respect for human rights, and so on, one wonders why these same countries totally ignore these principles when it comes to the operation of the international systems, which they control. There is practically no international organisation which is even-handed enough to take up the defence of the poor of the world. Economic globalisation without global governance systems is tantamount to delivering the countries and economies of the Third World to a small clique of countries, companies and individuals who control the world economy and will continue doing so for quite some time. In the absence of such governance it will be difficult for our governments in the South to abandon their traditional role of helping their people tackle issues of abject poverty, unemployment, illiteracy and disease.

An interesting quote from Kenichi Ohmae's book, 'The Borderless World: Power and Strategies in the Interlinked Economy', castigates those countries which resist the onslaught of globalisation, warning that they:

'discourage investment and impoverish their people. Worse, they commit their people to isolation from the emerging world economy, which in turn dooms them to a downward spiral of frustrated hopes and industrial stagnation. By looking outward with almost paranoid suspicion, fearing that exploiters will make off with whatever of value, they ignore the needs of their people and destroy the value – the human capital – their people represent.'

89

It is doubtful whether he would have written these words in the aftermath of what has happened to South East Asia and, now, Russia. It is no wonder that Malaysian Prime Minister Mahathir Mohammad, whose country has been on the receiving end of the ruthless effects of globalisation, takes a very different view of the situation:

> 'Today tens of millions of workers have lost their jobs, thousands of companies have been bankrupted, banks and finance companies have closed down, taking with them the deposits of their clients. Today millions of people are without food and medicine. Today governments are unable to function, much less to help the suffering masses. Today shops are looted, people are raped and killed. And all these things and more are happening because our governments have to be disciplined, to be forced to become transparent, to remove obstructions to the free flow of foreign capital, to the purchase and control by foreigners of national banks and businesses.... Globalisation is a great idea whose time has come. But it must be interpreted correctly if it is going to bring about a better world. Presently we are not too convinced that it is going to be good for us in the developing countries.'

Dr Mahathir points out that the source of the suffering of the developing nations is foreign:

> 'Who are the market forces? Certainly they are not local. These market forces are foreign, located in some countries where they cannot be seen. Taking advantage of their ability to breach borders with their capital they are able to devalue currencies at will.'

It is clear from the foregoing that responsible governments cannot realistically allow unbridled globalisation to take place without a measure of control and direction. It is important to note that Dr Mahathir does not reject globalisation out of hand. Indeed he welcomes it, only pointing out that at the moment it is a process that is running amok, destroying whole economies and people's aspirations.

It is interesting that even the greatest economies of this world are not wholly shielded from some of the nefarious effects of globalisation. Japan, whose economy is second only to the that of America, has felt these consequences and is currently having to grapple with a tough situation. Recently the chief of the US Federal Reserve, Alan Greenspan acknowledged that the American economy could not enjoy immunity from the effects of falling stock prices. 'It is just not credible that the Unites States can remain an oasis of prosperity unaffected by a world that is experiencing greatly increased stress'.

The issue of regulation comes up quite often in this debate. Even given that globalisation is here to stay, some thinkers believe that it is necessary to institute some measure of control to parry against the more negative effects of globalisation. What is being called for is some system of international governance agreed upon by all the players in the world economy.

What kind of regulation is required? Who will regulate and how? Lester Thurow, in his book, 'The Future of Capitalism: How Today's Economic Forces Shape Tomorrow's World', puts forward the point that globalisation takes national economic decisions from national decision makers and puts them in the hands of forces beyond the national boundaries. 'With internationalization national governments lose many of their traditional levers of economic control'.

But there is no agreement as to what kind of governance at global level should come in to take over the role progressively relinquished by the state. Thurow underscores this lack of agreement:

> 'To make a global economy work requires giving up a substantial degree of sovereignty, but the political Left and Right are both correct when they argue that this is undemocratic. It is undemocratic rule by foreigners or, even worse, rule by international bureaucrats. It could only be democratic if there were an elected government, yet the Left and the Right would be the first ones to reject any such government.

> 'As a result, for some period of time the world economy game will be played in an environment where the rules are in flux – and not clearly known. Even when they are written and known it is not clear who will enforce them'.

This kind of statement gives credence to Dr Mahathir's position, which calls for the gradual integration of the world economy, for caution in the globalisation processes so as to avoid the sudden shocks of the type that rocked his country and others.

Growing regionalisation

The formation of regional groupings may be the intelligent thing to do if weaker nations want to strengthen their participation in the global economy and international governance in order to avert or soften the more unpalatable effects of globalisation. Indeed, regionalism is fast becoming a new governance order. In our region the rise of groupings such as the East African Cooperation (EAC) and the Southern Africa Development Council (SADC) signals the currency of this trend. There is evidence of renewed vigour in these organisations, which, while not creating a superstate, do provide a number of agencies which complement national governments in handling certain issues which can only be tackled at regional level. It is through such organisations that problems of drug trafficking, arms running, environmental destruction and international terrorism and crime generally can be fought in a concerted manner. Recently this was demonstrated when police organisations from the SADC member countries collaborated in searching for and apprehending cars which were allegedly stolen within the region. The EAC has already launched a regional passport for nationals of the three countries and there is talk of establishing a regional parliament and a regional currency as well as agreeing coordinated policies on monetary and fiscal matters and investment strategies.

The intensification of global integration creates certain opportunities for malefactors of all sorts. Instant communication, supersonic travel, unprecedented access to knowledge and all the wonders of the technological revolution are not available only to those who mean well. Criminals too have access to them.

Regional groupings have also shown a willingness to act in concert to deal with issues related to security and governance, such as when ECOWAS, the West African economic grouping sent a multinational force into Liberia and Sierra Leone or when, more recently, some SADC member countries sent troops into Congo.

It would be extremely difficult for individual national governments to deal with increasingly sophisticated cartels of international drug smugglers, or cross-border arms dealers, drug traffickers and money launderers. As the criminal gangs become more sophisticated, it is imperative that those countries affected by their misdeeds coordinate their efforts to counter them.

The inadequacy of international organisations

Any discussion of global governance systems must touch on the status of present day universal organisations to evaluate their efficacy and the ability to act as truly representative world bodies mediating relations between competing interests in an increasingly integrated world. The weaknesses inherent in the United Nations Organisation are too well known to need elaboration here, but suffice to say that more and more voices are being raised now in favour of reform of the UN. Still all indications are that the United States is not likely to let go the unchallenged position it has acquired in the wake of the demise of the Soviet Union. The glaring inequality inherent in the Security Council veto and the powerlessness of smaller powers render the UN ineffective as a global institution for global governance. The World Bank and the International Monetary Fund are no more democratic and increasingly dictate terms to impoverished countries which have no choice but to follow their prescriptions on 'structural adjustment' even when these occasion extreme suffering to the peoples of the countries concerned.

Global capital is by nature elusive. It cannot be regulated by national legislation and supraterritorial legislation has not yet been created. With the free, unfettered movement of capital and relocation of factories in countries of the investor's choice, labour union activism has lost out. Workers are forced to accept otherwise unacceptable wages and other conditions because capital has the choice to go elsewhere. Alongside the weakening of labour movements because of the change in the nature of production from extractive and heavy industry to more sophisticated technological industries, needing fewer workers, we now have states unwilling to legislate in defence of their own people. This makes for an irresponsible capitalist order, which has rolled back the achievements of the labour movement in many countries over the last century. What is more it has meant the worsening exploitation of the weaker members of Third World societies, women and children, who have become virtual slaves of the NIKE syndrome.

International and regional organisations have not demonstrated great commitment to changing this obviously unacceptable situation. The defence of the hapless workers caught up in this disadvantageous situation has been largely left to activists of non-governmental organisations. Only the European Parliament has managed to include in its treaty a Social Charter designed to ensure respect for certain principles pertaining to labour. And even then we know that an acrimonious debate preceded that inclusion.

Other actors

The relative withdrawal of the state from certain traditional activities has brought in new actors who have taken up the advocacy of a certain number of issues, which are currently considered to be beyond the purview of the state. Thousands of non-governmental organisations have been set up to unite people with similar interests, and the voices of these NGOs have been gaining in strength worldwide as they seek to coordinate their activities and programmes. Figures given by Jan Aart Scholte in a recent paper show that the Union of International Unions boasts at least 15,000 institutional transborder members. The number of NGOs with consultative status at the UN rose from 270 in 1972 to 1200 in 1993, whereas more and more nationally based organisations are active in issues and causes with international dimensions such as disarmament, women's and children's rights, the environment and the rights of minorities. The growing strength of these human networks is sure to have a significant input into the emerging forms of international governance, as people outside government contribute energetically to the elaboration of the world agenda. Still, these organisations remain marginal and cannot for the time being be considered strong enough to provide the basis for true global governance.

Supraterritoriality and subsidiarity

Juxtaposed, the two concepts of supraterritoriality and subsidiarity could suggest a certain conflict. The notion that the world has become one place and that all of us have to march to the same rhythm might seem to preclude the idea that what is local takes precedence over all else. The apparent contradiction must be explained in terms of an emerging world system which does not as yet fit with what has been. The new is still struggling to gain acceptance while the old seeks to hold out until it gets answers to its queries, or gets swept away by irresistible force.

These are uncertain times and there are no ready-made answers because, as pointed out above, the world is still in flux and the present situation is likely to continue for quite some time. Meanwhile our efforts to better the lot of our people and develop our countries must continue.

It has been argued above that we are not about to witness the withering away of the state in the classical Marxist sense. Rather the modern state will have to adapt to new realities, adopt new strategies and forge new partnerships enabling it to remain relevant in a fast changing world.

The challenges are daunting. The level of competitiveness is such that disorganised and absent-minded states will be terribly marginalised even as the world is globalising. If serious efforts are not made to keep up, if we let globalisation happen to us instead of participating actively in its realisation, the chances are that we will be leading our people into a new and more insidious colonialism.

It is not only the highly advanced nations that we are faced up with. New and vigorous powerhouses have sprung up over the past three decades and, their current problems notwithstanding, they are fast joining a club whose exclusive membership can only take place at the expense of laggards. Recent experience would tend to show that even in the area of the so-called South-South cooperation those who cannot clearly identify their interests and fight to secure them will be ripped off.

Thus, even as we grapple with the problematic of global governance, we must accept the principle of subsidiarity, that governance, like charity, begins at home. As global citizenship is still within the realm of the desirable, local responsibility must constitute the base from which we seek the universal.

Reinventing government

If it is true that government is not disappearing, it is also true that its nature and role have to undergo significant transformation. The weak nations of the world need to invest in a new type of government that can take on the daunting challenges of globalisation without abdicating its responsibility. This is a government that takes cognizance of the new realities in a changing world and leads its people in sharpening their understanding of the forces in play, defining their interests and working tirelessly to secure them. There must be a realisation that left on their own, individual operators cannot compete against their counterparts in developed countries and those of the emerging economies which have stored up considerable momentum in the past thirty or so years. Government can, and should use its diplomatic channels to advance the interests of its constituents and give them protection in their dealings with foreign interests. Relieved of its former involvement in business, government finds itself free to act as coordinator, facilitator and regulator, encouraging initiative and defining parameters within which the different stakeholders are called upon to operate. Far from disappearing, this kind of government will be very much present, only its role will be different and more delicate, which requires intelligent and committed leadership.

Leadership as a crucial factor

As pointed out above, these are uncertain times, with more questions being posed than there are answers. In times like these, the question of leadership assumes critical importance. A lackadaisical, insouciant, inept or corrupt leadership is dangerous. What is needed is a leadership that is coherent and cohesive, one that possesses a vision capable of firing the imagination of the people and encouraging them to make sacrifices to achieve certain fundamental objectives whose realisation would bring real development. The complexities of the modern world, the competitiveness to which we are subjected, the pace of technological development and its impact on our relations with the developed world, themselves already unequal, all indicate that we need leaders who can lead rather than rule, both as individuals and as teams. Under the 'diktat' of the IMF conditionalities and the crushing debt burden our people are called upon to make sacrifices toward the common good. But it will not be possible for long to call on the people to sacrifice if they perceive their leadership as uncaring and corrupt. Even as we rail against the economic North we must not forget that within the South we have an economic North and that this North is made up partly of a corrupt and avaricious leadership which uses its positions to entrench itself in power so that it may continue to pillage our countries' wealth.

This necessarily brings to fore the issue of the fight against corruption. It is generally recognized that crime is inimical to development because it wastes resources, distorts relationships and can cause social instability. And yet it does not appear as if there is enough commitment to the fight against this canker eating away at the very soul of the nation. Good governance is an impossibility where corruption has become pervasive. It is impossible for the poor and weak to have a meaningful and fulfilling life. It is impossible to dispence justice. Real economic development will remain forever an illusion. In these conditions peace and stability cannot be guaranteed for long. It is imperative then for every nation to make a serious commitment to the anti-corruption struggle, not as an occasional witch-hunt to get at this or that individual or to settle political scores, but as a cultural stream running through our educational, administrative, political and civic landscapes, inoculating our societies against possible disintegration.

Intelligent democratisation

One of the hallmarks of the current intensification of globalisation has been a campaign of democratisation that has come as a result of constructs and prescriptions largely imported wholesale from the North. As multilateral organisations and donor countries have predicated economic assistance on performance in the area of governance many countries of the South have adopted formats of democratisation that may have little bearing on the historical, sociological and cultural realities of their societies. This has led us to adopt programmes such as multipartyism without adapting them to our local situations, as if it were possible to have a universal format to fit all cases. The mechanical application of these constructs has left us with bureaucratic and wasteful dispensations that have spawned more problems than solutions without introducing real participatory democracy in any significant way. What I am saying here is that multipartyism has not delivered democracy, and whereas the principle of free adhesion to an organisation of one's choice must remain unassailable we have to look beyond the existence of parties and work toward the promotion of a truly open and inclusive political culture, wherein all citizens will participate fully in decision making. There is definitely something wrong, and even dangerous, in a political dispensation, which is based on parties that in the end offer little choice to the electorate because the parties are simply contraptions for power grabbing. This kind of system has little to recommend it if those in power consider those in opposition as enemies, and vice versa.

What is required is the creative engineering of a system, based on the voluntary adhesion of all the people in a nation, and in different communities, based on solidarity and community of interest, where political parties are informed by a desire to advance the people's welfare rather than promoting the narrow and egotistical interests of a phalanx of corrupt, power-hungry politicians and other power brokers. Those in power must be prepared to effect thorough-going devolution, giving more decision-making powers to local entities, along with the power to raise finances and spend on local development programmes. It will not do to continue talking about the importance of local government if the centre still clings to all the powers and only delegates peripheral powers to the local authorities.

Civil society

All this will be difficult to attain without the existence of a strong and vibrant civil society, which allows as many people as possible to participate in the governance of their communities and nation. Lamentably civil societies in most developing countries are still weak and their contribution has not been spectacular except in a few countries and concerning certain issues, such as where trade unions have moved from the simple advocacy of syndical interests to influencing political trends. But trade unions and farmers' cooperatives are likely to be hurt by current trends in globalisation as Northern capital and markets use their versatility to maximize profits on the one hand and to keep prices down on the other. In countries where workers are seen to have been overprotected it may soon be a matter for the government to choose between removing that protection or losing investment.

Churches and other religious organisations have increasingly taken up the issues of human rights, the rule of law, land rights, minority rights and corruption and their voice has been effective in making governments pay heed. They have also taken up, with the international community, the issue of debt, and by networking with their colleagues in other countries they have achieved appreciable impact.

But perhaps one of the most important areas of civil society is that of the media. Globalisation has meant that the powerful media of the North have made their impact felt in an unprecedented manner. It is now no exaggeration to say that the world is informed by CNN. This development has led to the world being all wired up together, so that the plight of Aung San Suu Kyi in Myanmar or the struggles of landless peasants in Chiapas come to our living rooms with an immediacy and freshness which galvanize our attention like never before, and make their struggles, in a way, ours. At the same time the onslaught of cultural imperialism is taking its toll on our youth as they are daily bombarded with blatant consumerism promoted through television and radio programmes that glorify wanton sex, drug abuse and the quest for the green buck. Our societies have been delivered to the altar of the cult of Coca-Cola, Michael Jackson and Barbie. Our nascent local media have not found the intelligence to resist, and instead have accepted the role of amplifiers of these alien and frankly destructive values, as they echo whatever comes from the North without much thought. This cultural penetration is a necessary component of general globalisation, which uses our weakness to make our countries unthinking appendages of a world system in which we are required to play the role of buffoon. We are enjoined to reject this. As pointed out above, globalisation can only make sense for us if some of the ideas are fed into that process are ours, if we are consciously contributing to the culture of the world. Our media must take upon themselves the task of refusing this cultural brutalization.

This said, it is true that we are witnessing the emergence of vigorous media which have already, even in their infancy, made a great contribution toward better governance, exposing corruption in high places and demanding greater accountability from those in power. This has had a salutary effect on the politics of this country, especially in light of the demonstrated weakness of the party political system. What needs to be done now is to help the nascent media enhance their professional competence, raise their ethical standards and identify their place vis-à-vis the global media so that they may be able to input qualitatively into world processes as full and conscious participants.

Conclusion

The rapid transformations taking place in the wake of globalisation will modify the way we conduct business in a changed world. The way we govern ourselves and the way we relate to others are already changing and will continue to change at an even faster pace. It is not possible to live in isolation, even if that is what we wanted. The interconnectedness of the world has seen to that. From our weak position, which is caused by our inability to heave ourselves out of the mire of economic and social backwardness, we cannot realistically give ourselves much choice about whether or not to participate. Increasingly the countries of the North, on whom we have allowed ourselves to depend for everything, are breathing down our necks, prompting us to democratize here, liberalize there, observe rights here, fight corruption there, and so on. It is as if we do not know what is good for us without the North telling us.

But we can do something about our condition. We can resolve to organize ourselves with a view to harnessing our human and material resources for the development of our countries and participating in the globalisation processes as partners and not as choppers of wood and drawers of water. We must refuse any inferior station, and the only way for our refusal to have sense and impact is by intelligent and hard work.

GLOBALIZATION AND POPULAR RESISTANCE

Issa G. Shivji

Contradictory perspectives on globalisation

The phenomenon

It has been said often enough that globalisation is creating a global village or that we are living in the era of 'global interdependency' or 'global neighbourhood' (see Commission of Global Governance, 1995). This is meant to convey the message that national boundaries are breaking down as goods, services, finance, culture, ideologies and messages stream across boundaries invading every nook and cranny of the globe, flattening down diversity and idiosyncrasies in the process. Distances are being shrunk as time gets computed in split seconds. It is said that the very location of thinking, conceptualizing, acting and changing has shifted from nation-societies to the globe itself. The concept of space, say the pundits, is neither geographical nor social and much less national; rather it is cyberspace. In other words, to paraphrase Marx, time is annihilating space (Marx 1858: 524).

One writer summarizes the phenomenon of globalisation as follows:

> As the term is understood here, then globalisation refers to the emergence and spread of a supraterritorial, transworld dimension of social relations. In institutional terms, the process has unfolded through the proliferation and growth of so-called 'transnational' corporations, popular associations and regulatory agencies (sometimes alternatively termed global companies, global civil society and global regimes, respectively). Ecologically, globalisation has taken place in the shape of planetary climate change, atmospheric ozone depletion, worldwide epidemics and the decline of Earth's biodiversity, amongst other things. Economically, in what Karl Marx anticipated as capital's 'annihilation of space by time' (1857-8:524), globality has been realised *inter alia* in twenty-four-hour round-the-world

101

financial markets, transworld production lines and a host of global consumption articles. Normatively, globalisation has occurred through the expansion of worldwide standards (e.g., common scales of measurement and so-called universal human rights) as well as through networks of collective solidarity that spans multiple countries (e.g., amongst women, the disabled or indigenous peoples). Psychologically, globalisation has developed through growing consciousness of the world as a single space, awareness reinforced by everyday experiences of diet, music and dress, as well as photographs from outer space showing planet Earth as one location. In these various ways, the rise of supraterritoriality has been comprehensive, in some form and to some degree spanning all aspects of social relations (Scholte 1998:3-4)

That this revolution is fundamentally transforming the lives and conditions of the globe's five billion plus inhabitants, there is no doubt. It is the direction of the transformation and its ultimate outcome which are contested and which form the contending discourses on globalisation.

In what follows I will briefly discuss these under two broad sets of views which may be conveniently described as the dominant and the critical discourse.

The dominant discourse

The dominant discourse on globalisation is essentially celebratory. By and large, although perhaps dressed in new garbs, the broad theoretical and ideological framework and underpinnings are neoliberal. Spearheaded by mainstream economists, its analytical categories are all too familiar – free market, efficiency, economic rationality, comparative advantage, growth, etc. The site of its analysis is microeconomic and its epistemology is grounded in ahistorical empiricism of the statistical kind. Its research is focused on policy, i.e. prescriptive as opposed to academic or critical (diagnostic) which it often derides.

The central element of this discourse in Africa has been the state-market polarity or dichotomy. Abstracted from its historical concreteness, the ideal type of both the state and the market and their relationship are seen as those in Europe and North America. As the argument has it, the best and most efficient allocation of resources is the invisible hand of the market while the state has the function (functionalist paradigm) of creating an enabling environment and playing its 'traditional' role of maintaining law and order. By 'traditional' is meant what is supposed to have happened in the developed Northeast. Once this is subjected to history, however, the traditional role attributed to state turns out to be an ideological make-believe as the state has always played a very central and interventionist role in the processes of capitalist accumulation worldwide (Baran, 1957) and is doing so now on the global level in the interest of its own transnationals as witnessed, for example, in the policies pursued by the US and the OECD countries in such world forums as the WTO, etc. (see Third World Network, *Third World Resurgence* Issues).

The institutional home of many of the leading spokespersons of this discourse are the employees and consultants of the WB/IMF/WTO triad. In Africa, the manifestation of the discourse is even more programmatic, and prescriptive rather than theoretical. A significant number of African economists who matter are hired to operationalize the liberalization/marketization/privatization policies and de-statization of their countries economies taking the form of structural adjustment programmes whether 'imported' or 'home-grown', meaning locally assembled. (see Lipumba et. al., 1984; World Bank, 1994; Gibbon, ed., 1993; Gibbon, ed., 1995). If such consultants indulge in academic discourse at all it is celebratory or eclectically critical at best (see, for instance, Msambichaka et. al., 1994).

The furthest the 'critical' perspective within the dominant discourse goes is to argue that globalisation is inevitable and here to stay; that it offers 'opportunities and challenges' and that African policy-makers should make every effort to find a niche in the process (1998 NAM Declaration, see also South Commission, 1990). The choice is not so much between globalisation and no-globalisation but rather to be globalized or to globalize. In other words, in ideological terms, blatant neoliberalism is given a social democratic face where the free market is tempered with what Karlsson calls the 'social market' (1997) (whatever that means in conceptual and practical terms) and structural adjustment is given a human face by creating social safety valves.

The issue, however, remains that eclectic softening of prescriptions derived from the basic paradigms of neoliberalism and the devastating results of global reach of capitalism does not even scratch the surface of the real issues embedded in the political economy of the new forms (perhaps a new stage?) of capitalism and imperialism represented by globalisation. The discourse remains imprisoned within the strongly ideological paradigms and categories of neoliberalism or pragmatic prescriptions of the 'if-you-can't-beat-it-join-it type' (Furedi 1993).

I now turn to more critical perspectives on globalisation.

Critical perspectives

Critical perspectives on globalisation, particularly in the South, may be classified between those which are explicitly political and constructed around the ideologies of resistance and those which are of a more scholarly kind with their genesis in the theoretical frameworks of neo-Marxism or neo-dependencia. The common theme of the critical discourse is to demonstrate the extreme polarization, inequalities and inequities generated by the so-called process of globalisation on the one hand, and the ruinous effect it has on the livelihoods, environment and ecology of the planet, on the other (see, for example, Brecher & Costello, 1994; Korten, 1995; *Third World Resurgence*, various issues). Demonstrating the extreme income inequality at the global level by a graph in the shape of a champagne glass (see figure), Korten computes that '20% of the world's people who live in the world's wealthiest countries receive 82.7 percent of the world's income; only 1.4 percent of the world's income goes to the 20 percent who live in the world's poorest countries.' (Korten *ibid.*: 106). In a word, these critical perspectives argue that the single central element of the process of globalisation is the globalising of poverty and concentration of wealth, power and control over production and communication in the hands of a few hundred giant corporations (see Kim, 1997) and, now, one must add, global financial speculators in the image of George Soros.

Radical political economy approaches

The approaches and perspectives within this larger framework may differ in their nuances and details but some of their salient points may be summarized in outline as follows:

1. Globalisation is seen as part of the worldwide historical process of the expansion of capital or the process of accumulation on the

world scale (Amin, 1995; Toussaint, 1998) destroying national and local spaces as sites of accumulation and reconstructing societies. Marx himself foresaw this although he could not have even dreamt of electronic finance involving trillions of dollars every day. 'Capital by its nature drives beyond every spatial barrier. Thus the creation of the physical conditions of exchange – of the means of communication and transport – the annihilation of space by time – becomes an extraordinary necessity for it.' (Marx, 1858: 524)

2. The central form of capital in the current process of this trend called globalisation is the tyranny of finance capital, which has taken a particular form in worldwide financial markets or electronic finance. This is a new form compared to the rise of the finance capital as analyzed by Hobson and Lenin.

3. Globalisation has immensely accentuated the extreme polarisation inherent in the process of capital accumulation worldwide, concentration of capital on the one hand and poverty on the other. Under globalisation this is not simply a process of proletarianization or peasantization as under classical capitalism but that of marginalization which throws out millions from any productive activity or exertion of labour power in any form. It creates not only the reserve army of adults and children, but what Marcos calls, 'disposable population' of street children and totally unemployed human wreckage (Marcos, 1997; Brecher & Costello, 1994).

4. Globalisation further accentuates the processes of concentration and centralization of capital in very few corporations and people on a global level, who are not bounded by geographical, national and social spaces or jurisdictions, and who control production, exchange and distribution at the touch of a computer key. This is very well illustrated by the new rules or regimes (TRIPs, TRIMs, MAI, E-commerce etc.) that the hegemonic states and corporations of the US and Western Europe have managed, and are continuing to incorporate in WTO agreements (see various issues of *Third World Resurgence*).

5. The social polarization of classes on a world level goes hand in hand with fusion of social and political power and obliteration of the distinction between corporate and state structures and

institutions: a global military-industrial-financial complex.

6. Globalisation fuses and begins to obliterate the distinctions between speculative and productive capital on the one hand, and 'illegal' and legal capital on the other hand, as small states starved of capital encourage offshore money laundering which in turn is converted into legal capital through overground banks.

7. Globalisation gives the triad of highly undemocratic world financial institutions, the WB/IMF/WTO unprecedented powers reminiscent of the conquering and plundering states of the early centuries.

8. These writers posit varied processes as opposing the tendencies inherent in globalisation such as (a) a polycentric world (Amin, 1995); (b) globalisation from below (Brecher & Costillo, 1994; (c) popular and social struggles across national boundaries.

One more recent articulation, which presents globalisation as a new form of militarisation and conquest of territories reminiscent of the old conquests of the Third World, deserves some mention. It crystallizes the premises postulated above in a graphic language, albeit somewhat overdramatized.

Globalisation as militarisation

Subcomandante Insurgente Marcos of the Zapatista Army of National Liberation (Mexico) argues that 'Modern globalisation, neoliberalism as a global system, should be understood as a new war of conquest for territories.' (Marcos, 1997:1). The end of the 'Cold War', or the Third World War, as Marcos calls it, did not mean the end of war. As a matter of fact, the end of the Cold War signified the beginning of a new war, World War IV. 'This required, as do all wars, a redefinition of national states, the world order returned to the old epochs of the conquests of America, Africa and Oceania.' And in the process the national state was reduced to a 'department of a neoliberal megacompany' (*ibid.* 4). Figures showing sales of large corporations exceeding the GDP of many a small country are now common place. 'General Motors' 1992 sales revenues (USD 133 billion) roughly equalled the combined GNP of Tanzania, Ethiopia, Nepal, Bangladesh, Zaire, Uganda, Nigeria, Kenya, and Pakistan. Five hundred and fifty million people inhabit these countries, a tenth of the world's population.' (Korten, 199: 220-21).

In his militarist imagery, Marcos observes that at the end of the Cold War capitalism produced the marvel of a neutron bomb whose 'virtue' is that it only destroys life while leaving buildings intact. 'But a new bellicose 'marvel' would be discovered at the same time as the birth of the Fourth World War: the financial bomb.' (*ibid.*: 4) The recent crash of some East Asian countries no doubt illustrates the power of the financial bomb and this was, perhaps, only a dress rehearsal.

In neoliberalism, Marcos posits, the state is reduced to the bare minimum:

> 'In the cabaret of globalisation, the state shows itself as a table dancer that strips of everything until it is left with only the minimum indispensable garments: the repressive force. With its material base destroyed, its possibilities of sovereignty annulled, its political classes blurred, nation states become, more or less rapidly, a security apparatus for the megacorporations that neoliberalism builds in the development of this Fourth World War.' (*ibid.*:15)

As a matter of fact, Marcos chips in, even the monopoly of violence, the traditional characteristic of the state, is put on sale by the modem market spurned by globalisation.

The global jigsaw puzzle, in the imagery employed by Marcos, is summarised thus:

> 'The first is the double accumulation, of wealth and poverty, at the two poles of global society. The other is the total exploitation of the totality of the world. The third is the migrant part of humanity. The fourth is the nauseating relationship between crime and power. The fifth is the violence of the state. The sixth is the mystery of megapolitics. The seventh is the multi-forms of pockets of resistance of humanity against neoliberalism.'

It is the 'pockets of resistance ... of all sizes, of all colours, of the most varied forms' which we turn to in our next section.

State-civil society-community or pockets of resistance

> The empire of financial pockets confronts
> the rebellion of the pockets of resistance.
> Subcomandante Marcos

The problematic of civil society

The concept of civil society came into vogue in the 1980s with the impending collapse of the Soviet and East European systems and the democratisation drive in Africa (White 1994). In Eastern Europe, following the collapse of bureaucratic socialist regimes (or actually existing socialism, as they were then christened), the construction of civil societies was seen as returning to "normal society" on the Western model", as the editors of the *Journal of Democracy* would see it (Journal of Democracy, January 1996, 'Civil Society after Communism', p.11). In Eastern Europe itself, the term has been used in as many different ways as contexts (see *ibid*. p. 18, exchange between President Havel and Prime Minister Klaus of the Czech Republic).

The discourse on civil society in Africa too has used the term with all kinds of meanings from associational connotations ('civil societies') to all-virtuous, harmonious social space (see, for instance, the International Peace Academy Publication 'Civil Society and Conflict Management in Africa', 1996). It is probably the US based Africanists, whose earlier modernization constructs had been shattered by dependencia-underdevelopment theorists, that took to the term with a vengeance (see Mamdani 1990 & 1995). Abstracted from European history itself where the concept was first generated, and from actually existing social struggles in Africa to which it was being applied, the term civil society in the Africanist hands became a sterile state-civil-society bipolarity (Mamdani 1990 & 1995 *ibid*).

Again, not unusually within Africa and among African scholars, the civil society political science discourse has tended to revolve around the state-society bipolarity constructed as it is in the image, and under the influence, of American political science. However, it has had one interesting 'home-grown' twist and that is using the term to signify autonomy and freedom of associational life, that is, autonomous of state institutions. Thus the argument for the construction of civil society, at

108

least in the first phases of democratisation, was overwhelmingly constructed around the freedom to form autonomous organisations – associations, people's organisations (POs), mass organisations like trade unions etc. (Shivji 1984, Shivji ed. 1986, Kiondo 1993, Gyimah-Boadi 1996).

Within this as well there were two perspectives and contradictory currents. In the more radical current, freedom to organize, while being a reaction to statism of the previous decades, was also seen as a site of social struggles. In the more conventional current, however, the perspective veered towards more institutional and managerial dimensions. These contradictory perspectives perhaps bring out a fundamental epistemological and methodological difference on the state-society dichotomy and which, indeed, in my view, is one of the basic theoretical flaws of the Africanist conceptualization of state-civil society paradigm.

Analyzed historically, the concept of civil society in European history represented the transition from medieval feudalist to capitalist society. In that context civil society was, both for Hegel and Marx (and even perhaps Weber), for example, an ensemble of free, equal, abstract individuals associating in the public sphere of production as opposed to the private sphere of the family. For Marx, therefore, civil society was synonymous with bourgeois society. The concept is developed in opposition to feudal relations where the public and the private are merged and statuses are determined by birth and privileges, where politics is direct 'that is to say, the elements of civil life, for example, property, or the family, or the mode of labour, were raised to the level of political life in the form of seignority, estates, and corporations.' (quoted in Sayers 1991:75).

At the same time for Marx (and this is directly relevant to our conceptual debate on civil society), whereas civil society presents itself as an ensemble of free individuals and as a separate sphere from state/politics, it is, as a matter of fact, the soil from which arises, and in which is embedded, state power. Two things must be noted from this: (a) that the individualism and freedom associated with that in civil society are abstract beings; that once the *social being* of the individuals is examined it becomes clear that civil society is neither homogenous nor free but rather an ensemble of contradictory social relations. (b) That there is no wall between the state and the civil society because social power is the harbinger of, and in turn is secured by, political power, the state.

In short, the state-civil society discourse, abstracted from European history on the one hand, and actually existing social and political struggles in Africa on the other, gives us a singularly flawed conceptual framework which in turn generates, at best, an irrelevant research agenda and takes us even further from understanding the reality of how history is made and who makes it.

Pockets and forms of resistance

It is important to keep the conceptual flaws discussed in the last section in mind so as to appreciate a number of other bipolarities in this discourse and their implications for our work. For example, the concept of 'civil society' is often presented in contrast to 'traditional' society, which polarization in turn leads to many modernization prescriptions with little relevance to historically constituted 'traditional' societies.

But even more important is the political diagnosis which result from such bipolarities. On the one hand, the resistance and struggles of the people are not recognized because they do not take the form of modern struggles of civil society (e.g., trade unions, chamber of commerce, NGOs etc.), or worse, are condemned as primordial, illegitimate or backward (fundamentalist, tribalist etc.) This, of course, has an impact not only in understanding the forms and ideologies of resistance of the people to various forces impinging on them (including the apparently faceless ones advocated by WTO etc., such as markets, investments, patent laws on biodiversity etc.) but, how, in turn such struggles and resistance restructure, or could restructure, the institutions/apparatuses of the state. We thus deprive ourselves of an important piece of locally generated knowledge, values and cultures.

It is these types of theoretical perspectives which, for example, caused two important African research bodies – the Third World Forum and CODESRIA – to mount research agendas on Popular Struggles and Social Movements respectively (see Nyongo, ed. 1987 & Mamdani & Wamba eds. 1995). These efforts have considerably taken the African discourse beyond the state-civil society polarity and may be more useful in helping us to elicit the impact of globalisation and the resistance to it in our own concrete situation. The kind of struggles documented in these studies also occur in Tanzania. In one form or the other people thus resist the impact of globalisation. However, not much sustained research has been done in the country to unravel how people organize their resistance using their own material, spiritual and traditional, as well as civil, organisational resources. I will briefly cite two examples, to illustrate some of these points.

NAFCO vs the Barabaig

The National Agriculture and Food Corporation (NAFCO) was established as a state corporation in 1969. Around 1970, with aid from the Canadian International Development Agency (CIDA), the government entered into a gargantuan project called the Tanzania-Canadian Wheat Project. The area that was identified is situated on the Basotu Plains in the Hanang district of the Arusha region. This area belongs to the Barabaig or Datoga people who are agro-pastoralists and some among them (including the Iraqw and Somali) had also developed successful middle-level wheat farming (Raikes 1971).

Over 100,000 acres of land was alienated to NAFCO without consultation of the communities concerned and without even following the procedures provided in existing law. For example, a witness in the case of *Mulbadaw vs NAFCO* (High Court Civil Case No. 10 of 1981 at Arusha) described the procedures of alienating peasant and pastoral land as follows:

> 'When we start a project the peasants are informed through the instruments of the Government and the Party. A letter is written from NAFCO Headquarters to the regional Party Chairman who was then also the Regional Commissioner. He then spreads the message to the villagers through the *Katibu Kata* [ward secretary], etc. The NAFCO Manager in the area also assists in the spread of the information. In the 1980/81 season we had to move people out. The procedure followed was to inform the *Katibu Kata* of the affected area. On 29 March 1979 I saw the *Katibu Kata* to instruct him to move out the peasants who were in the area earmarked for expansion.' [quoted in Shivji 1998, 10)

The description is not untypical. This is how things were done during the heyday of the one-party system with directives coming from the top and people just informed to make way of what went under the guise of a 'national project' or a project in 'public interest' (Shivji 1990 *passim*)

The project has had enormous adverse effects on the community as they have lost their pasturelands, resulting in the decimation of their herds. The large-scale prairie-type farming has also resulted in the destruction of trees and other vegetation affecting rain patterns and soil erosion (Lane 1996). Meanwhile, the relationship between NAFCO and the surrounding community has been one of hostility and antagonism. Incidences of abuse of human rights, the beating and arrest of pastoralists, and confiscation of cattle on the pretext of trespass has been common (Shivji & Tenga 1985, Shivji 1990, Kisanga Commission 1993).

The Barabaig people have not simply taken this oppression sitting down. During the one-party era they used party channels open to them, while in the early eighties a number of court cases were opened. In the late eighties they formed their own civil organisations and NGOs. With the help of researchers and other activists their case was publicized, particularly in Canada, resulting finally in the appointment of a government commission (Kisanga Commission 1993) to investigate human rights abuses (for the campaign see Lane 1996, 165 et. seq.). So, available civil society avenues of struggle have been explored. One of the more interesting forms of struggle, however, which I have not seen seriously researched into and documented, is the struggle of the Barabaig women for their community's land.

A story in a newspaper a couple of years ago (citation misplaced) reported that Barabaig women held an 'only women' traditional meeting in the forest to pressurize their men to fight for their land. Apparently, this type of meeting is part of the tradition of the Barabaig people. Women meet, discuss and adopt resolutions and do not return to the villages until their deliberations are done. It is said, they also have their own sanctions against their men, such as boycotting household chores, to ensure enforcement of their decisions.

NCAA vs the Maasai

The Ngorongoro Conservation Area Authority is a statutory body, which oversees the famous Ngorongoro Conservation Area (NCA). NCA covers some 60% of the Ngorongoro district and has over 50,000 Maasai residents (based on Shivji & Kapinga 1998). The residents were shifted to the Ngorongoro plains when Serengeti was created as a national park in the late fifties, with a written agreement from the then colonial government that their interests would be paramount in the new area.

Since the creation of the conservation area, Maasai residents have had a running battle against the Authority as more and more of their rights have been curbed. In particular, they have a deep-seated grievance since 1975, when cultivation was prohibited in the Area by law.

The NCAA has such enormous powers of governance, law-making and enforcement and supervision over the residents that it can in effect be considered a governmental body. Yet the residents over whom these powers are exercised – and there are many instances of abuse of power as well – have no representation in the Authority. As a matter of fact, where the by-laws of the Authority conflict with those of the District Council (local government), those of the Authority prevail. In effect, therefore, the Maasai are literally disenfranchised in that they lack citizen's rights to be represented in 'local government'.

Over thirty years now the Maasai have been resisting and fighting for their land rights and other human rights, their rights to participate in making conservation policies and generally for their right to be part of the governance structures directly affecting them. In this they have very effectively and systematically used their traditional Maasai structure of Laigwenak (traditional Maasai elders) to ensure legitimacy and accountability. They have combined the traditional leadership and accountability structures with modern civil NGOs and other means of national and international campaigning to publicize their plight. Again, this form of struggle and resistance has not been studied in any great depth.

These two case studies, which are not untypical, bring out several strands, which need to be further explored. In both cases, the usual justification for forcibly integrating the communities in the so-called processes of globalisation is in terms of some or the other so-called developmentalist ideology of modernization, with both the Barabaig and the Maasai presented as 'backward' people. Nationally, statist top-down approaches have prevailed to the exclusion of the democratic process of participation and consultation. Internationally, the 'magic wand' of foreign investment as the agency of development has been waved incessantly in spite of evidence to the contrary. For example, studies have shown that the Tanzania-Canadian Wheat Project has been a story of failure, from whatever point of view – environmental, economic, etc. – it is assessed (Lane 1996, *passim*).

The studies also indicate that there are processes of resistance on the ground which seem to combine skilfully available civil forms of resistance with traditional forms of legitimacy and organisation. But, given the ultimate statist, modernist, developmentalist and donor-driven biases in the conceptual framework of research, these remain under-researched.

Preliminary conclusions and approaches to setting a research agenda

Our brief discussion in this paper leads us to identify the following broad topics and approaches to setting a research agenda in the area of globalisation and popular resistance.

1. To understand the processes of globalisation, its impact on the people and the 'role of civil society' in the process of transformation, we need to generate a rigorous conceptual/ theoretical framework. Therefore, issue must be joined with contending discourses on globalisation so as to crystallize basic theoretical guides and this should be part of any basic research agenda. In other words, the generating of theoretical knowledge should not be considered the monopoly of the intellectuals and researchers of the North alone. Intellectuals and researchers in Africa need to intervene consciously in this process.

2. The guidelines so generated would in turn guide and, in the process be refined by, basic empirical research on the impact of globalisation on the lives and livelihoods of the vast majority of people (e.g., land, environment, biodiversity and its 'traditional' uses, etc.) (see URT, 1992). By and large, over the last ten or fifteen years, basic research on what exactly is happening in, and to, our societies has virtually ceased as paid consultancies and pragmatic policy-making have taken over the time and intellectual resources of some of our best brains. Any serious research organisation has to plan and make a conscious contribution towards reversing this trend.

3. The impact of globalisation is not simply one-sided but people defend and resist it in various organisational forms and through various ideological prisms ('pockets of resistance'). The process of

domination and resistance in turn generates structures of state governance which need to be closely analyzed as well as their potential for restructuring of our state and civil society institutions explored. This calls for basic research on *actually existing struggles* beyond the more visible, the so-called modern, civil society struggles.

The theories, practices and pragmatism of the globalisation-modernization paradigm have hitherto proved to be a great failure in understanding changes on the one hand, and helping to produce pointers in the direction of desirable change on the other. The result is to throw up one's hands in lamentation over the crisis of theory or, more commonly, to appear to act pragmatically by advocating jumping on the bandwagon: 'Globalisation is the reality, it is inevitable and cannot be challenged. There is nothing that can be done except to join it'! This is partly because the said intellectuals and researchers themselves are deficient in their knowledge and understanding of how people in their everyday lives deploy their indigenous resources to resist adversity and adverse changes in their societies. It is at the strategic inter-face of understanding change and helping to guide it that the role of basic research should be located.

References

Amin, S. (1990), *Maldevelopment: Anatomy of a Global Failure*, Zed, London.

Amin, S. (1993), 'The Issue of Democracy in the Contemporary Third World' in Gills *et al.* (eds.), *infra*. pp. 59-79.

Amin, S. (1995), 'The Future of Socialism' in Barry Gills & Shahid Qadir, (eds.) *Regimes in Crisis*, Zed, London.

Baran, P. (1957), *The Political Economy of Growth*, Monthly Review, New York.

Brecher, J & Costello, T. (1994), *Global Village or Global Pillage*, South End, Boston.

Baxi, U. (1996), '"Global Neighbourhood" and the "Universal Otherhood": Notes on the Report of the Commission on Global Governance'*, Alternatives 21: 525-549.

Foley, M. & Edwards, B. (1996), *The Paradox of Civil Society*, Journal of Democracy, vol. 7, No.3: 3852.

Furedi, F. (1995), *The New Ideology of Imperialism*, Pluto, London.

Gills, B., Rocamora, J. & Wilson, R. (eds.) (1993), *Low Intensity Democracy: Political Power in the New World Order*, Pluto, London.

Gibbon, P. (ed.) (1993), *Social Change and Economic Reform in Africa*, Nordic Institute, Uppsala.

Gibbon, P. (ed.) (1995), *Liberalised Development in Tanzania*, Nordic Institute, Uppsala.

Gyimah-Boadi, E. (1996), *Civil Society in Africa*, Journal of Democracy, vol. 7, No. 2, 118-132.

Havel, V. & Klaus (1996), *Civil Society after Communism*, Journal of Democracy, vol. 7, no.1, 12-23.

International Peace Academy (1996), *Civil Society and Conflict Management in Africa: a Report.*

Khor, Martin (1997}, *SEA Currency Turmoil Renews Concern on Financial Speculation*, Third World Resurgence, No. 86, October 1997.

Kiondo, A. (1993), 'Structural Adjustment and Non-Governmental Organisations in Tanzania: A Case Study', Nordic Institute. Uppsala, in Gibbon, (ed.) *supra*, (1993).

Korten, David C. (1995), *When the Corporations Rule the World*, Kumarian, Connecticut.

Karlsson, M. (1997), *Globalisation, Africa and New Realities*, report of a lecture given by M. Karlsson, ESRF, Dar es Salaam.

Kisanga Commission (1993), *Report of the Commission on Violations of Human Rights in NAFCO Wheat Farms Hanang District*, Dar es Salaam, mimeo (a Government Commission).

Krahl, A. (1998), *"Southern Perspectives" on Globalisation: A Foray into the Socioeconomic and Socio-political Literature*, Institute of Social Studies, mimeo.

Lane, Charles (1996), *Pastures Lost: Barabaig Economy, Resource Tenure, and the Alienation of their Land in Tanzania*, Initiatives Publishers, Nairobi.

Lipumba, N. *et al.* (eds.) (1984), *Economic Stabilisation Policies in Tanzania*, Economics Department, University of Dar es Salaam.

Mafeje, Archie (1995), 'Theory of Democracy and the African Discourse: Breaking Bread with my Fellow travellers' in E. Chole & J. Ibrahim, (eds.) *Democratisation Processes in Africa*, Dakar: CODESRIA, pp. 5-28.

Marx, K. 1858 (1973), Penguin, Grundisse.

Mamdani, M. (1987), 'Contradictory Class Perspectives on the Question of Democracy: the Case of Uganda' in Peter Anyang' Nyong'o, (ed.) *Popular Struggles for Democracy in Africa*, pp. 78-95, Zed, London.

Mamdani, M. (1990), *A Glimpse of African Studies Made in USA*, CODESRIA Bulletin, (1990)/2.

Mamdani, M. & Wamba, E. (eds.) (1995), *African Studies in Social Movements and Democracy*, CODESRIA, Dakar.

Marcos, I. (1997), *Neoliberalism* [This document appeared in a European publication and was translated by Cecilia Rodriguez of NCDM: page nos. from e-mail printout in the author's possession.]

Msambichaka, L. *et al.* (eds.) (1994), *Development Challenges and Strategies for Tanzania*, DUP, Dar es Salaam.

Nyongo, A. (ed.), 1987, *Popular Struggles for Democracy in Africa*, London, Zed.

Nyerere, J. K. (1993), 'Life is a Basic Right' *Daily News*, 27/09/93.

Nyerere, J. K. (1994), 'Address to UN General Assembly on UN Agenda on Development' *Daily News*, 20/06/94.

Our Global Neighbourhood (1995), Report of the Commission on Global Governance, Oxford.

Raikes, P. (1971), 'Wheat Production and the Development of Capitalism in North Iraqw', reprinted in L. Cliffe *et al.* (eds.), *Rural Co-operation in Tanzania*, Tanzanian Publishing House, Dar es Salaam.

Sayers, D. (1991), *Capitalism & Modernity: An excursus on Marx and Weber*, Routledge, London.

Scholte, J. (1998), *Globalisation and Social Change*, Transnational Associations, 1/1998 & 2/1998.

Shivji, Issa G. (1984), *The Reorganisation of the State and the Working People in Tanzania*, in Socialism in the World.

Shivji, I. G. & R. W. Tenga (1985), *Ujamaa in Court*, Africa Events, vol. 1, No.2.

Shivji, Issa G. (ed.) (1986), *The State and the Working Class in Tanzania*, CODESRIA, Dakar, Senegal.

Shivji, Issa G. (1990), *State Coercion and Freedom in Tanzania*, Lesotho, Rome.

Shivji, I. & Kapinga, W. (1998), *Maasai Rights in Ngorongoro*, IIED, London.

Shivji, Issa G. (1998), *Not Yet Democracy: Reforming Land Tenure in Tanzania*, IIED, London, Faculty of Law & HAKIARDHI, Dar es Salaam.

South Commission (1990), *The Challenge to the South*, OUP, London.

Third World Network, *Third World Resurgence,* Issues 81/82, 46, 77/78, 85, 84, 95, 90/91.

Toussaint, E. (ed) (1998), "La bourse ou la vie", *La France Contre les Peuples Brussels,* 8:396

URT (Tanzania) (1994), *Report of the Presidential Commission of Enquiry into Land Matters*, Scandinavian Institute of African Studies, Uppsala.

White, G. (1994), *Civil Society, Democratisation and Development (1): Clearing the Analytical Ground in Democratisation,* vol.1, no.3, 375-390.

World Bank (1994), *Adjustment in Africa: Reforms, Results, and the Road Ahead*, Oxford University Press, London.

LOCAL PERSPECTIVES ON GLOBALIZATION: THE CULTURAL DOMAIN

Penina Mlama

Introduction

The cultural domain of globalisation in Africa is probably the most complex to grasp compared to the other socioeconomic dynamics of globalisation. Indeed, as it has historically been the case, it may also be the most neglected. This, however, does not diminish the powers of culture to negate or facilitate the development of a society in the context of globalisation.

Cognizant of the delivery of definitions of culture, the discussion herein is constructed around an understanding of culture as 'a people's way of life', the perception and manner of doing things that not only identifies a people but also sets a particular framework and standard of behaviour and self esteem for a decent socioeconomic survival of a society.

A construction of culture

First is the society's own vision of what constitutes an ideally decent socioeconomic structure for its survival. The vision is framed around the basic evolutionary drives that foster life in order to maintain order and continuity. These include food, shelter, safety and procreation. The framework of the vision is in addition influenced by such other factors as geographical location, climate, innovations and so on. Secondly, systems of behavioural patterns, ideas, beliefs, values and attitudes to enshrine that vision come into place. These become the guidelines on which the members of society then relate to each other and to their environment. Deserving to belong to the society means abiding by the dictates of these systems. These systems regulate social behaviour, including individual behaviour driven by self-interest versus communal behaviour.

People pick up their society's behavioural patterns, ideas, beliefs, values and attitudes through socialization. Societies, however, do not leave the cultural moulding of their people to chance. Specific institutions are set up to inculcate, reinforce and foster the accepted behaviour, beliefs, values and attitudes. Education, religion, art and communication are some such institutions. From childhood, a person's perception of life in terms of what is good or bad, acceptable or unacceptable, desirable or undesirable is directly or indirectly formed and influenced by the educational curricula, the tenets of the religion practised, the images and messages of art and the communication media.

In order to ensure its survival, a society expects conformity to its defined systems of behavioural patterns, beliefs, values and attitudes. A system of conformity in the form of both rewards and sanctions is therefore normally instituted. Those whose behaviour adheres to what is expected by the society are normally rewarded through material gains, status or ceremony. The renegades are subjected to sanctions including reprimand, humiliation, exclusion, isolation and other forms of punishment. Various levels of regulatory bodies and legal systems are put in place to effect the sanctions.

Culture needs to be understood as a web of all these factors; the society's vision of what it is and should be, its ensuing systems of behavioural patterns, ideas, beliefs, values and attitudes to support that vision, the institutions to effect the systems and a system of conformity.

A historical perspective on globalisation

Globalisation for Africa should not be delinked from the other historical processes of Africa's relationship to the rest of the world. The slave trade, colonialism, neocolonialism, imperialism and, the Cold War constitute the parentage of today's so called globalisation. In each of these eras Africa was in a disadvantaged position as a victim of political, economic and social exploitation. The continent's power for self-determination has been severely and systematically eroded. The slave trader, the colonial master, transnational corporations, the Western and Eastern blocs have over the years significantly weakened the very foundation of Africa's existence.

The rubble from this continued onslaught is the fragmented and fragile economic structures that have given Africa the now seemingly irreversible character of poverty. The trauma from this over century-long exploitation is manifested in the 'circuses' in Africa's political arena ranging from dictatorships, empires, military regimes, pseudo-multiparty democracies to sheer anarchy. Intensified poverty, starvation, war and genocide are but a few spots of the ugly face of Africa's long history of exploitation by both internal and external forces.

Globalisation should be viewed within this historical context, and the enthusiasm often accorded to globalisation should not blur the realities of Africa's past sufferings. Indeed this history should provide lessons to better handle the forces of globalisation.

The historical context of globalisation is very significant in reviewing culture. As explained in the introduction, if culture is taken as a 'peoples way of life' interlinking a vision of what a society thinks it is or should be and systems and institutions that ensure the attainment of the vision, then the first problem to confront is whether Africa has ever had a chance to determine its way of life. It does not require too complicated an analysis to show the difficulties Africa has had in formulating its vision and determining its own way of life in the face of the forces of slave trade, colonialism, neocolonialism, imperialism or the Cold War. The situation may not be much different, in fact it seems more difficult in the context of globalisation.

A more specific view, however, will see culture as a dynamic process and therefore whatever this history brought to Africa should be seen as part of the dynamics of the continent's existence. While this position is not refuted, it is important to take note of the fact that these forces of slave trade, colonialism, imperialism and the Cold War were dominant and oppressive in character and did not always stand for the interests of African people. A contradiction is therefore encountered when Africa incorporates, without question, this externally formulated cultural dynamic of oppression and domination into its accepted way of life.

A look at many African countries, however, indicates a powerlessness to deal with the cultural complexity arising out of this history. It is no wonder that the debate on African identity has seen no resolution in sight. Another manifestation is the lack of any defined cultural policies in many African governments. For example, it took Tanzania thirty-seven years after independence to institute a cultural policy, passed by Parliament in 1998. Many African governments also display a lack of clarity on what to do with the cultural sector. Culture is always the sector which governments do not know where to place. For example, between 1961 and 1998 in Tanzania, culture moved from one ministry to another nine times, its partners spanning from Community Development, Youth, Labour, Education, the Prime Minister's Office and Sports. A discussion of culture and globalisation in Africa must, therefore, take into account this history of systematic negation of the African culture and its resultant confusion and inability of the Africans to determine their way of life.

Globalisation and its implications for culture in Africa

Globalisation has triggered some trends that are bound to affect the cultural outlook of the world. For example, the world is seemingly being drawn into a single economic system. This is accompanied by an intensification of the accumulation of capital, the monopoly of production by a few multinational companies and, the manipulation of labour markets by supraterritorial production networks.

The world has also become distanceless due to the rapid development of information technology. The production and dissemination of knowledge and information are controlled by global information and communication networks that can reach the whole world in an instance.

The sovereignty and autonomy of nation-states are significantly eroded through the control of their economies by transnational institutions such as the IMF and the World Bank. Indeed, the heavy indebtedness of African countries has left many governments voiceless.

For Africa, globalisation increases the historical complexity of its culture and the cultural domain has to reflect these global dynamics. It is clear, for example, that self-determination is even more difficult under globalisation than it was under, say, colonialism. Then, African societies attempted to put up resistance against the imposition of a European way of life. That is why some definite forms of African identities survived decades of European influence even though the European way of life became eventually dominant. This was possible because in fighting colonialism, the African at least knew who the enemy was. The European colonial master used the open system of the school, the church, the mission and the sisal plantation to impose the European way of life. People could take the option to circumvent or avoid these institutions and maintain their way of life, although not always with maximum success due to the impossibility of stopping cultural dynamics.

122

Under globalisation however, Africa is dealing with a multi-faced and sometimes elusive monster. The face of structural adjustment, for example, brings with it devastating effects on socioeconomic structures. Globally controlled information and knowledge production networks are the cultural face that aggressively disseminates behaviour patterns, values and attitudes that have left African youth culturally confused.

The face of Western-modelled multiparty democracy has expanded political participation but has often divided the people into intensely rival political camps with little gain for the masses of voters.

Global human rights and natural justice activism have challenged the legitimacy of oppressive forces but have often provided a convenient loophole for corruption in the legal arena where everything seems to go as law under the so-called 'natural justice'. Civil society has ushered in hundreds of NGOs, both secular and religious, that have formed a new network of economic and spiritual exploitation of the people. Where is Africa's dignity in those multitudes of frenzied, tearful worshippers as they shout at the top of their voices in prayer? What culture is this that believes the problems of unemployment, disease or poverty can be solved through frenzied prayer? What have these global networks of evangelism or fundamentalism to offer to better the quality of life for Africans? What work ethics do we inculcate in the youth of these sects who believe that any problem will be solved simply by praying?

There is also no denying that the forces of globalisation are powerful, and often incomprehensible. It is even scary that most African leadership does not display much comprehension of the risks to their nations from globalisation. For example it is pathetic how ministers of finance or development planning flag national government budgets or development plans which in essence are IMF, World Bank conditionalities. The leadership has lost even the courage to explain to the masses why the government cannot challenge these conditionalities even in the wake of so-called democracy.

And when members of parliament, who the masses have entrusted with the responsibility to guard national interests, dare not question the legitimacy of these externally determined policies and plans that threaten the country's very existence, indeed, when as in the case of Tanzania, MPs profusely congratulate the minister of finance or of planning and even celebrate parliamentary endorsement of these pseudo budgets and plans, then 'the circus' is no longer funny. Something is very wrong, somewhere. What culture is this, which sits back and idly watches external forces destroying its people?

Globalisation is effectively taking away from Africa the power for self-termination and Africa, especially its leadership, seems oblivious or incapable or indifferent or resigned to the global forces at play. In many cases, the leadership chooses to abandon the African ship and board the global ship from which, with the help of the global forces, they have embarked on the pursuit of self-interest. They leave the African masses swim or sink with the African ship.

Whatever interpretation one takes, the danger for the African cultural context is that globalisation is eroding Africa's ability to formulate and institute a vision of what it is and what it should be. Africa is losing the power to define, influence or control its own way of life.

With this loss of vision, the very foundation on which a people's culture is constructed is shaken. The inevitable result is cultural confusion. There is no firm foundation on which to construct the behavioural patterns, ideas, beliefs, values and attitudes on which people's economic, political, social character can be based. As such anything goes. For example, in many indigenous African cultures behavioural patterns stressed hard work. A person's standing in the society was gauged on his or her ability to work hard and produce enough food for survival. The economic success of leadership was measured on the facilitation of economic opportunities for the people. A chief for example, had to make sure everyone had land on which to grow food for their family. Today, some people work very hard; others do not work at all and the rewards often go to those who do not work. Indeed, those who can get rich without working hard or through trickery are considered the 'smart guys'.

It is also not clear how many millions of able-bodied and trained young people should fill the streets before the leadership decides to put the issue of youth unemployment on its agenda. In Tanzania for example, the government is instead, contemplating extending the retirement age[43]. In many African cultures a young man was not considered fit to get married if he was not adequately engaged economically. What regulations will the marriage institution set today for its massive unemployed young men and women? And what kind of work ethic does a society instil in someone with no opportunity for employment?

The dynamics of globalisation make it extremely difficult to construct a location-based vision of a society's way of life. But meanwhile the opening up of borders to the global influence ushers in all sorts of cultural systems, to fill in the vacuum. For example, the behavioural patterns of the urban youth are becoming homogenous worldwide through the influence of the television, video, the CD, jeans, Nike and Coca-Cola. And the global drug barons are also creating a global generation of drug users. Parents are often totally confused about how to raise their children. This is to say nothing of the behavioural patterns of the parents themselves most of whom have lost legitimacy as parental role models. Adults, teachers, religious leaders, and political leaders, who are normally the guardians of a society's identity, seem to have lost their sense of direction. The glamour of global forces and the global life styles pulls them in different directions. Corruption, promiscuity, violence, theft or sheer hooliganism are no longer exceptional behaviour among adults. The increase in broken marriages, child sex abuse, rampant child neglect within homes are producing a physically, mentally and psychologically affected generation of young people.

It is indeed very ironical that these unfortunate behaviour patterns are intensified by globalisation which, on the other hand, is seen as having opened up Africa to democracy, human rights, and freedom of speech. Political practice, especially election campaigns in some African countries became intensely corrupt with the introduction of multi-party democracy. Domestic violence and rape has reached alarming proportions alongside increased activism for human rights. It became imperative for Tanzania to pass the Sexual Offence Bill in 1998 in an attempt to curb this trend. Corruption in government circles is sitting side by side with policy statements on transparency and good governance.

The same people who are vehemently preaching human rights and natural justice have turned justice into a commodity sold to the highest bidder regardless of who is accused or the complainant. What are the

---

[43] The retirement age of public employees has been extended since the writing of this paper (editors).

cultural pillars on which to mould peoples' behaviour?

Education systems, which are normally the strongholds of a society's cultural values and attitudes, are often in disarray. Local education systems, whose curricula were carefully constructed to incorporate national pride and ethics, are being sidelined by IMF/World Bank conditionalities that say the social sector is not productive and should therefore not be state-supported. At the same time, they are being sidelined by stiff competition with schools and universities of the North. Parents, especially leaders, are competing in sending their children to study in the North in search of a global curricula and eventually global employment opportunities but hardly check whether the so-called global curricula include Africa. For which life are these African children being educated and for which values and attitudes? Or is globalisation value-free and as such African children will remain African even if they spend their prime years in Europe or America?

The disintegration of local education systems through the effects of structural adjustment and IMF/World Bank conditionalities have introduced dynamics in the schools detrimental to the role of the school as a cultural institution. The poorly paid teacher now looks at a student as a commodity and not a ward to be nurtured and moulded into a decent citizen. The teacher is no longer the guardian and role model of a society's morals, values and attitudes.

Like the parent, the teacher is also no longer clear of what constitutes the morals, values and attitudes of society. Cases of students beating or abusing teachers, burning school property, teachers sexually abusing students, teachers refusing to teach students who have not paid them unofficial tuition fees, children dying in boarding schools because teachers have not attended to their sickness, ministry officials demanding gifts from the already meagre resources allocated to schools, and drug abuse among students are just some of the unfortunate trends that render many schools unfit as cultural institutions.

Religion poses another perspective of the cultural crisis in Africa. The intensification of poverty under globalisation is leading many people, especially the young and women, to search for the meaning of life in religion, especially in religious fundamentalism. The numerous religious sects in Africa and the multitudes of their followers are a sad manifestation of the failure to grapple with socioeconomic forces and a resort to the spiritual. Globalisation's global communication networks has facilitated the easy spread of these religions and the strengthening of solidarity of the sects across the globe. It is not surprising that fundamentalism in both Christianity and Islam is spreading like wildfire. Through cable television believers in Africa are accessed by preachers from Korea, Japan, the USA and Germany. Whereas in the past religious teachings were based on the values and attitudes of the dominant cultures from which the religion emerged, the cultural boundaries are getting blurred in these global religious trends. Religion no longer necessarily espouses what one particular society thinks is right or wrong. It resides more and more at the level of the supernatural. As opposed to the traditional religions, the local context is no longer the reference point. In Tanzania, for example, families have been torn apart by Christian fundamentalists, who have cut links with their parents or spouses because they are 'saved' and therefore, it is not proper for them to associate with the 'unsaved'. Childcare has suffered because parents are spending too many hours praying, including overnight wakes. The young have dropped out of school and shunned employment in the name of evangelism and the belief that once you are saved, everything in life will work out. Parents are under constant fear for their children not only because of the problems of early pregnancy, HIV or unemployment, but also of religious fundamentalism.

Governments, however, turn a blind eye to these trends on the argument that they have no religion and the constitution espouses freedom of religious association. But what is the impact of this religious fervour on the socioeconomic welfare of the society? What morals, values, attitudes and ethics are imposed on these believers, especially the young?

It is clear that the dynamics of globalisation have added new dimensions to the cultural context, not only into Africa but in the whole world. It is for this reason that the UNESCO World Commission on Culture and Development in its report *Our Creative Diversity* (Perez de Cuellar; 1995) recommends a need for global ethics to try to give direction to the emergence of a global culture. The main elements of such a global ethics are mentioned as human rights and responsibilities, democracy and the elements of civil society, protection of minorities, commitment to peaceful conflict resolution and fair negotiation, and equity within and between generations. It is recommended that these be the principle basic ideas to furnish the minimal standards and political community should observe.

It is not the intention of this paper to discuss these recommendations but rather to note the need for communities at local level to realize that the dynamics of globalisation demand some kind of action by which to guide the concerned community into the future.

Some ideas on the way forward

So far this paper has concentrated on the negative trends of globalisation. This is not to say that there are no positive developments. Indeed the opening up of the world has created new opportunities in terms of markets, skills acquisition, access to information and knowledge. Tanzania is more able now than ever before to compare itself to the rest of the world and to try to aim higher in its search for an improved quality of life. Competition for markets has also increased production and entrepreneurial creativity.

It has been argued that global practices in human rights, democracy, gender equality, have penetrated many parts of the world and accelerated/influenced the elimination of oppressive practices. Tanzania has been similarly influenced with positive results. The expansion of civil society activities, the introduction of multipartyism in 1992, and the 1998 Sexual Offence Bill are but a few manifestation of the positive trends of globalisation.

We wish to argue here though that, in general, Tanzania has hardly started to address globalisation as an important factor for its future direction. That is the first problem that needs serious attention. Tanzania must first and foremost strive to understand what globalisation is all about, and what its implications are to all facets of life and to the socioeconomic development of the country. It is from such a broad understanding of globalisation that the economic, social and cultural context can be properly understood and a realistic vision of what Tanzania wants can be set out.

Since the country is in the process of formulating the 2025 vision, it is hoped that globalisation will receive adequate attention[44].

---

[44] The Vision 2025 document was produced shortly after this paper was prepared (editors).

In the cultural domain, the next step would be to identify the behavioural patterns, beliefs, values and attitudes to espouse the tenets of the country's vision. However, before any attempt is made to suggest any direction in this rather tricky area it is necessary to study the existing situation. What are the behavioural patterns, beliefs, values and attitudes on the ground today? Are these desirable or not? Can they or should they be changed? Who is setting the pace? This will require extensive study on how the various groups in society relate to each other at home, the workplace, at school, and on the street and in other public places. The young, adults, parents, children, the aged, leaders and professionals in urban and rural areas are responding to the forces of globalisation in ways that require to be understood. A historical perspective on the changes will also be important in order to project into the future.

The second area of study would be the institutions that are normally the transmitters of cultural values and attitudes, including schools, the mass media, religion, the arts and other socialization processes. What changes have emerged in these institutions, what new forms have they taken? Have new institutions come into existence? Who controls these institutions and to what effect? What is their social status and their ability to mould people culturally? Are the traditional institutions withstanding the global impact on culture?

A third area would be a study of the systems of conformity. What are the new forms of reward or sanction for cultural conformity? Are there any systems at all or have they all simply disintegrated. Is it possible or desirable to institute any regulatory processes or should it be a free for all? Is it desirable to have national cultural standards or not? What should be the limit between what is acceptable nationally and globally? Who sets the standards? Have indigenous systems been completely marginalised?

As shown above these are all important questions. It is our opinion that globalisation in Tanzania has not received sufficient attention in the past to provide answers to these questions. As such they should be subject of research towards creating a clearer understanding of the cultural context of globalisation in Tanzania.

The major issue of concern, however, is: can Tanzania, or any African country, for that matter, be a significant player in influencing or controlling the global forces at play?

References

Alonso-Gaomo *et al.* (1997), *Globalisation and Growth Prospects in Arab Countries,* IMF Working Paper.

Craig, G. and Mayo, M. (eds.) (1995), *Community Empowerment. A Reader in Participation and Development,* ZED Books, London.

Daris, Rob (1997) *Perspectives on Globalisation and Regionalization: a view from South Africa,* Institute of Development Studies, University of Dar es Salaam.

Dubbeldam, L. (ed.) (1995), *Values and Value Education,* CESO Paperback No. 25, The Hague.

Gonzalez, D. (1997) *Who leads where? African Leadership in the XXI Century,* International Conference on Leadership in Africa, IDS, Dar es Salaam.

Knutsson, K. (ed.) (1998), *Culture and Human Development,* The Royal Academy of Letters, History & Antiquities, Stockholm.

Krahl, A. (1998), *'Southern' Perspectives on Globalisation: a Foray into the Socioeconomic and Socio-political Literature,* Institute of Social Studies, The Hague.

Perez de Cuellar, J. (1995), *Our Creative Diversity: Report of the World Commission on Culture and Development,* UNESCO Publishing/Oxford & IBH Publishing.

Scholte, J.A. (1998), *Globalisation and Social Change,* Part I & Part II, Transnational Associations, 2-69, 1/1998, pp.2-11; 12/1998, pp.62-79.

Urebvu, A.O. (1997), *Culture and Technology: A study of the 1997 theme World Decade for Cultural Development 1988-1997,* UNESCO, Paris Culture and Technology.

Wangwe, S. (1997), *Globalisation and Marginalization: Africa's Economic Challenges in the 21st Century.* International Conference on Leadership in Africa, IDS, Dar es Salaam.

THE NATURAL RESOURCES DOMAIN IN TANZANIA

Idris S. Kikula & Aida Kiangi

Introduction

The big leap in modern technologies has made transport, communication, etc. extremely easy. This has facilitated interactions between societies, cultures, individuals and institutions throughout the world. It has also intensified societal demands and hence pressures on the natural resource base and the environment in general. Because of the growth of world trade, pressure on resources in one corner of the world may come from many hundreds of miles away. For example pressure on an endangered plant species in Tanzania could originate from multinational pharmaceutical companies in America or Europe. The plant may have been reported to have therapeutic properties that are not known from any other source. This forces the company to move fast to come up with a monopoly of the drug.

It is clear that globalisation is being pushed by motives to maximize profits in trade. In this regard one can straight away see where developing countries stand. The business community and citizens of developing countries cannot compete on equal terms with their counterparts in the North in world trade that has become extremely rigorous and competitive. The North knows it has this competitive advantage and is all out to exploit the resources from developing countries as fast and as cheaply as possible. On the other hand international trade in natural resources has great potential not only for contributing to the economic welfare of the trading countries but also as a source of employment, which is increasingly becoming a serious problem. Widespread unemployment is bound to lead to insecurity and undermine law and order.

Globalisation has been facilitated by policies such as those of the World Bank, the IMF and the World Trade Organisation. The World Bank and the International Monetary Fund's insistence on Structural Adjustment Programmes (SAPs) is closely tied to free trade and the expansion of commerce through the deregulation of markets. This is also the mission of the World Trade Organisation. These policies are top-down and authoritative, so much so that developing countries are being told what to and what not to do even in their own 'backyards'. The economic structures and orientations of developing countries have been greatly influenced by these policies. In Tanzania for example, during the 1980s and 1990s, policies were dominated by responses to macroeconomic stabilisation: market reforms and increased external resource flows in order to revive economic growth in the medium term.

At the same time there is increased awareness of environment and sustainable development. As a result trade has been firmly linked to environmental issues. For example, Agenda 21 states that trade and environmental policies should be mutually supportive. The Agenda also outlines how environmental concerns and trade could be better integrated.

In this paper we attempt to relate this intensified globalisation to natural resources and the environment of Tanzania. There are a number of constraints to this endeavour. The first is that information on exports is extremely difficult to get. The responsible institutions in government, parastatals and even NGOs are reluctant to release information, for whatever reason. One is left to speculate on what is so confidential about the whole matter.

Where information is available it is in most cases badly coded, making it difficult to interpret. For example some of the commodities are not coded, making it difficult to know what they are. In other cases, different years have different coding systems. As such it is difficult to establish trends. Nevertheless we have tried to make the most of the information we have been able to acquire.

The second part of the paper provides an overview of the natural resource endowment of the country, to provide a framework for the subsequent sections in the paper. The third section is dedicated to the trading of selected natural resources. The resources that are selected for treatment here will hopefully provide an overview of what is going on. It is not easy to include everything here because the natural resource domain is broad. The fourth section looks at the implications of globalisation on the natural resource base. The last section of the paper points to potential areas for research.

The natural resource endowment

In order to appreciate the diverse nature of the trade in natural resources in Tanzania, it is important to be aware of the main features of the endowment. We outline the main natural resources below.

Tanzania is endowed with many natural resources that form the basis of global trade. It is probably proper to mention the agricultural base first because of its importance to the national economy. It is estimated that about 55% of the total land area has good potential for agriculture. The agricultural sector contributes about 46% to GDP and employs nearly 80% of the national workforce. Traditional agricultural exports include coffee, cotton, cashew nuts, sisal, tobacco and tea. Increasingly non-traditional agricultural and horticultural exports are becoming popular. However, some of them – like castor seeds – have been abandoned. It would be interesting to find out why. In Dodoma, for example, castor oil seeds were an important cash crop until the 1980s. But the crop is no longer being cultivated, narrowing the source of livelihood of the people in the area.

The coast of the Indian Ocean in the east of the country is 800 km long. The continental shelf ranges between 4 to 35 km wide with a total area of about 17,500 km^2 This area includes the famous islands of Unguja, Pemba, and Mafia. Many varieties of corals are to be found here. There are also proven offshore reserves of gas and possibly oil.

The deltas of the Rufiji, Pangani, Wami and Ruvuma rivers have extensive mangrove forests that support and sustain marine resources, such as prawns. Mangrove poles have exported to places as far away as the United Arab Emirates for centuries. During the last ten years the farming of algae for export has become an important economic activity for the coastal communities. The seaweed is mainly for export.

Lake Victoria, in the north, is an important source of freshwater fisheries. Nile perch hasvbeen the main commodity traded from this lake since 1970. Lake Tanganyika in the west and Lake Nyasa in the southwest are also important sources of freshwater resources, including ornamental fish. The river systems are a source of many export commodities, including crocodiles.

Forest resources

There is a high diversity of vegetation in Tanzania. Not only are there many habitats, but also a large number of species. There are about 250 families, over 10,645 species, over 927 subspecies, and over 1102 varieties of terrestrial flora. The Zambezian Region, of which Miombo forms the largest part, is reported to have over 8,500 species, giving it the most diverse flora in the whole of Africa (URT, 1997). Table 1 below gives estimates of the main categories of forest types in Tanzania.

Table 1. Estimated Areas of the Main Forest Types in Tanzania

Type of Forest	000 ha
Forests (other than mangrove forests	1400
Mangrove forests	80
Woodlands	42891
Total	44371

Source: Ministry of Natural Resources and Tourism (MNRT) (1994)

It should be noted that the above figures are only estimates because the situation is quite dynamic. But it will be seen from the table that despite the extensive deforestation that is taking place, there are still extensive areas that are covered by forests, woodlands and other land-cover types that provide habitats for wildlife. The different land-cover types are also unique ecosystems and sources of genetic resources. Forests are sources of timber and many other products, some of which are exported. Woodlands also provide important habitats for beekeeping from which honey and beeswax is harvested. Forests and woodlands include approximately 80 000 hectare of plantations.

The different land-cover types occur under different legal statuses. These are indicated in Table 2 below as follows:

Table 2. Estimated Areas under Different Legal Statuses

Legal Status	000 ha
Forest Reserves	13024
Forest/Woodlands within National Parks	2000
Non Reserved Forest Lands	29347
Total	44371

Currently most of the forests and woodlands are in forest reserves and protected areas. The non-reserved forestlands are quickly being opened up for cultivation. This situation is exacerbated by rapid population growth. Also, the high prices of agricultural inputs mean that people cannot afford them and they have to practice extensive farming.

Information on the contribution of forests to the national economy is not readily available, but 1988 estimates indicate a contribution of between 2 and 3 percent of GDP. However, these estimates seem to be low because of an unrealistic consideration of their contribution to the rural economy. For example the contribution of fuel wood is normally not considered.

It is also estimated that the forestry sector contributes approximately 10% of the country's registered exports and provides about 730,000 person-years of employment. The value of the Miombo Woodlands is estimated about USD 1,050 per hectare when wood, beekeeping, fruit, mushrooms, game meat, medicines and water conservation are considered together. The value of forests is however estimated at USD 750 per hectare based on royalties collected, exports and tourism earnings. At a global level Tanzanian forests are valued at USD 1,500 per hectare based on the recycling and fixing of carbon dioxide (URT, 1994).

Forests, woodlands and other land-cover types have many sources of value. These include non-forest products. The main types of non-forest products or minor forest products are shown in the table below:

Table 3. Examples of non-forest products

Types of Use	Product
Fibres	Bamboo, palm grasses, etc.
Foods	Nuts, edible fungi, spices, honey and game meat
Medicinal products	Various
Aromatic	Oils from sandalwood, junipers
Extracts	Tannins, dyes, latex, gums and resins e.g. gum Arabic
Others	Honey, beeswax etc.

Source: URT (1994)

Medicines as a minor forest product are also extremely important. Many people in the rural settings use traditional medicines for different types of treatments, including problems of the digestive system, genitourinary system, central nervous system, infections, etc. It has been shown that there are 405 identified plant species belonging to 257 genera, which are medicinal and are frequently used for the treatment of both animals and humans. The wide range of curative properties of Tanzanian flora has made it a major target for international pharmaceutical companies

Wildlife resources

The wildlife sector in Tanzania is now the second largest contributor to GDP and foreign exchange earner after agriculture. This is certainly a direct outcome of the great diversity of terrestrial vertebrates in the country, providing a great potential for wildlife trade. The main groups are amphibians, reptiles, birds, and mammals. Table 4 below provides information on the approximate number of species for each of the groups:

Table 4. Number of Species of Amphibians, Reptiles, Birds and Mammals in Tanzania

Group	Families	Genera	Species	Notes
Amphibians	10	36	133	Some of the species are endemic
Reptiles	21	104	293	
Birds			1065	2% are endemic, some are endangered
Mammals			302	13 species are endemic to Tanzania and Kenya
-bats			97	4 species are of conservation concern
- rodents			100	9 species are of conservation concern

Source: URT (1997)

Invertebrate species are also commodities of international trade. Table five below provides an estimate of the number of species for the main groups.

Table 5. Number of species of some selected Invertebrates in Tanzania

Group	Species	Notes
Isopods	677	3% are endemic
Millipedes	600-1000	many remain undescribed, about 40% are endemic
Butterflies	1235	

Source: URT (1997)

Tanzania is known for its commitment to the conservation of wildlife. One indication of this commitment is the size of land dedicated to wildlife conservation, which is about 25% of Tanzania's total surface area. These areas include National Parks, Game Reserves, Game Controlled Areas and the Ngorongoro Conservation Area. Table 6 below gives the land areas under the different categories of use.

Table 6. National Environmental Management Council (NEMC) (1993)

Category	Number	Area (Mill. ha)	% of total land
National Park	12	4.11	4.43
Conservation Area	1	0.83	0.93
Game Reserve	18	9.70	10.40
Proposed Game Reserve	12	-	-
Game Controlled Area	56	9.00	9.60
Total	99	23.64	25.36

It is important to note that the Serengeti and Kilimanjaro National Parks, Selous Game Reserve and the Ngorongoro Conservation Area have been classified as World Heritage Sites because of their importance. In addition, Serengeti, Kilimanjaro and Lake Manyara National Parks have been given the status of Biosphere Reserves. Lake Manyara National Park is also a Ramsar Site.

No consumptive use of national parks is allowed. They are

No consumptive use of national parks is allowed. They are specifically managed for non-consumptive uses, like research, tourism and education. On the other hand game reserves are managed for authorized consumptive and non-consumptive use of the wildlife resources. Grazing of livestock in game reserves is currently not allowed. The subject is however under serious discussions at an international level.

The Ngorongoro Conservation Area was established in 1959 for purposes of conservation and the traditional use of the Masaai. Game controlled areas are essentially wildlife spill areas and buffer zones for national parks. Wildlife Conservation Act No. 12 of 1974 regulates the consumptive use in these areas.

Mineral resources

There are vast deposits of mineral resources in Tanzania, including coal, iron, gold, diamonds and many others. The main gold fields are in Geita, Kahama, Musoma, Tarime, Chunya, and Mpanda. Vast coal and iron deposits are to be found in the Southern Highlands.

Trading in natural resources

Wildlife

Many natural resources and natural resource products are exported from Tanzania. As was mentioned in the first section, in this paper we have considered only selected examples. In Table 7 below, the trend of exports between 1978 and 1986 is shown. It will be noticed that, except for ivory, beeswax and diamonds, there was a general increase in the assortment of commodities exported during the period in question.

Table 7. Selected Export Commodities (Values in Tanzanian shillings. Where appropriate the quantities are indicated)

Commodity	1978	1979	1980	1981	1982	1983	1984	1985	1986
Bovine hides, dried	997	152	624	547	361	21	311	600	1224
Bovine hides, wet chrome	77	52	79	647	572	734	703	434	277
Lumber (M³)	1601	861	9901	3256	6939	606	2217	13681	2746
Ivory, elephant	26	14	14	3	10	2	12	11	17
Gum Arabic	361	314	428	144	217	129	97	470	384
Cinchona bark	65	123	84	152	108	161	119	167	161
Beeswax	189	354	217	437	197	61	96	90	106
Diamonds (non industrial)	68111	51105	62243	58218	56466	31693	58149	64793	38927

Source: Bureau of Statistics (1989)

139

It will be noted in Table 8 below that the mid 1980s saw diversification of the commodities brought onto the export market. For example the export of live animals and fish products was introduced and the value of exports increased which suggests that the volume also increased.

Table 8. Selected Domestic Exports (Millions of Tanzanian Shillings)

Commodity	1985	1986	1987	1988	1989	1990
Live animals	3	1	5	136	8	43
Meat products	0	10	0	3	10	1
Fish products	22	85	284	678	603	924
Hides and skins	40	53	270	355	637	862
Wood and cork	6	39	154	353	696	2477
Coal and cokes						1

Source: Bureau of Statistics (1997)

Tanzania exports more birds than any other country in Africa except Senegal. Bird populations worldwide are declining due to over-hunting, habitat destruction and trade. The USA and Europe are the largest international markets for birds. Currently 3.5 to 5 million birds are documented in the commercial bird trade. These include passerines (songbirds and finches) and psittacines (parrots, macaws, cockatoos, conures and parakeets). Five countries currently meeting the world demand for songbirds and parrots are Senegal, Tanzania, Argentina, Guyana and Indonesia. African countries supply most of the passerines and two thirds of all the species listed in CITES. Senegal is the largest single exporting country, with an estimated 4 million birds a year being exported (WCI, 1992).

Tanzania exports 300,000 wild birds annually, predominantly finches (including an average of 67,000 CITES species). Top export is the Fisher's Lovebird parrot (*Agapouris Fischeri*), which is endemic to the country, an estimated 54,000 of which are exported every year. There are indications that Fisher's Lovebird has a greatly reduced distribution compared to other birds endemic to Tanzania.

It should be noted that the actual number of birds taken annually may be larger than is reported due to deaths during capture, transportation, at holding grounds, during shipment to other countries and in quarantine on arrival. Many species are also traded illegally. Thus it is not easy to acquire the exact figures.

The quantity of live exports for 1997 is given in the table below.

Table 9. Live Animal, Ornamentals and Fish Exports for 1997 (in tons)

Commodity	Quantity
Live animals	759.8
Live ornamentals	7.5
Other live fish	14

Source: Bank of Tanzania

Chimpanzees, and Colobus and Mangabey monkeys are among the targets of illegal trade. With baby chimpanzees reported to fetch up to USD 20,000, it is a lucrative business which needs to be controlled through scientific procedures, which are invariably non-existent. Thus as it stands there is a lot of illegal trade, but it is going on undetected. Many other products are traded illegally, including rhino horns and ivory, which are very popular on the South East Asian markets. We hope that the discovery of the *Viagra* drug will eventually ease the pressure on the rhino horn and other similar products which are sought for their alleged aphrodisiac properties.

Table 10 below provides examples of exports of forest and beekeeping for 1989/90 and 1990/91. It will be noted in the table that the difference in the value of the forest products exported between 1989/90 and 1990/91 is relatively small. But most significant is that the quantities exported in the year 1990/91 were almost double those of the previous year. Most certainly, this indicates how the pricing of natural resources is biased against the exporting countries.

Table 10. Export of Forest and Beekeeping Products

Product	Unit	1989/90 Qty	1989/90 Value (000 USD)	1990/91 Qty	1990/91 Value (000 USD)
Logs (Indigenous)	M³	2945	1264.3	-	-
Logs (Plantation)	M³	5278	928.9	-	-
Subtotal		8223	2193.2	3991	798.3
Boards (Indigenous)	M³	1428	341.0		
Boards (Plantation)	M³	3658	392.3		
Subtotal	M³	5086	733.3	1649	338.6
Floorin	M³	1794	939.8	2125	1183.5
Blackwood	M³	47	677.3	55	682.1
Subtotal	M³	1843	1617.1	2180	1865.6
Subtotal Forest		15150	4543.7	7820	3002.5
Honey	Ton.	20.5	23.5	123	221.4
Beeswax	Ton.	260.9	662.7	696	2088.0
Subtotal Beekeeping		281.4	686.2	819	2309.4
GRAND TOTAL			5229.9		5311.9

Source: URT (1994).

Some selected commodities exported in 1995 are given in Table 11 below. Commodities that were included in the statistics but had not been classified have been omitted from the table. Notable from the table is the increase in the items included in the export list compared to the previous years. We notice for example the introduction of items such as frogs legs and intensification of the export of fish and fish products.

Table 11. Selected Exports for 1995

Commodity	Net kgs
Fowl (*Gallus domesticus*)	15,760
Other	682,954
Frogs legs	24
Ornamental fish	126,846
Trout	2,406
Sardines	204,373
Dog fish	100
Cod	12,972
Rock lobster	3,472,907
Coral	4,629
Fish ova	12,267

Source: BET (1998)

Further diversification of export products has included the export of live trees. According to the 1995 statistics from the Bank of Tanzania, approximately 21 tons of live trees and other plant parts (bulbs, roots, cuttings, flowers) were exported.

Table 12 below, based on 1997 data, shows the intensification of the export of non-traditional exports like flowers, wood charcoal and many other wood products. The information available clearly indicates that as the globalisation mood catches up with the process, the diversity of export products is increasing. This is also the case with the volumes exported.

Table 12. Exports from Forests for 1997 (in tons)

Commodity	Quantity
Live trees (bulbs, tubers, rhizomes)	9
Fresh cut flowers and buds	643
Gums and resins	3012
Fuel wood in logs and billets	1842
Wood charcoal	1200
Other tropical wood species	2836
Oakwood	0.3
Other wood	2830
Tropical veneer sheets	163
Statues and other ornaments of wood	375
Wood marquetry and caskets of wood	162
Cork and its articles	50

Source: Bank of Tanzania (1997)

As mentioned above with regard to non-traditional exports, Tanzania's trade policy advocates among other things the identification of new markets for non-traditional exports. The fisheries industry in Lake Victoria is one example of recent developments in non-traditional exports. Fish catches in the North of the world are declining and traders are looking increasingly to the South for an increased supply of this commodity, thus increasing the importance of fish trade between North and South.

This has resulted in an export-oriented fisheries industry, which in turn has profoundly affected the traditional fisheries industry and the different groups of people who depend on it. Although the trade is contributing to the national economy, it has threatened the food security and livelihood of traditional fishing communities.

Traditionally fisheries have almost always been dominated by small operators. Processing and trading involved to a large extent women from the fishing community. With the increase in the Nile Perch catches, the fisheries industry changed completely and policy changes had to be effected on the management of the fisheries industry. Table 13 provides an indication of the diversified nature of fish exports in 1997.

Table 13. Intensification of Exports of Fish for 1997 (tons)

Commodity	Quantity
Fresh or chilled trout	34
Frozen pacific	28
Frozen salmons	194
Fish or chilled fish fillet	4090
Frozen fish fillet	17465
Flour mills and pellets of fish for human consumption	135
Fish liver, eggs, (dried /smoked /enbrined)	30
Fish fillet (dried, salted, or enbrined but not smoked	109
Smoked herring including fillet	19
Smoked fish excluding herring and salmon	36
Dried fish (not smoked) excluding code	3266
Herring (salted or enbrined but dried or smoked	1
Other fish (salted or enbrined but not smoked or dried)	64
Fish ova	59

Source: Bank of Tanzania

The export of lobsters, prawns and crabs has also grown with time. The statistics for 1997 are given in table 14 below:

According to the statistics available at the bank of Tanzania, a total of 385 tons of corals, shells and natural sponges were exported in 1997.

Minerals

The mining industry in Tanzania is still relatively small and young. However it is growing fast following the economic liberalization policy. The government of Tanzania seems to be determined to ensure that the country's mineral endowment is effectively harnessed and contributes to the economic growth of the country.

Table 14. Exports of Lobsters, Prawns, Crabs etc. for 1997 (in tons)

Commodity	Quantity
Frozen rock lobster other than sea crayfish	0.7
Frozen lobster	42
Frozen shrimps and prawns	865
Frozen crabs	21
Frozen crustaceans including flour mills or pellets for human consumption	0.7
Lobsters (excluding frozen ones)	4
Crustaceans (not frozen) including flour/pellets/mills for human consumption	48.5
Mussels (excluding live/fresh or chilled)	5
Cattlefish and squids (live, fresh or chilled)	30.4
Octopus (live, fresh or chilled)	742
Snails (other than sea snails)	1
Aquatic invertebrates	124
Fish fat, oils and fractions	3

Source: Bank of Tanzania

Some of the recent instruments put in place to realize this goal include legislation for the mineral sector, which came into force in September 1998 under the Financial Laws (Miscellaneous Amendment) Act 1997 and the Tanzania Investment Act.

In October 1997 the Mineral Policy of Tanzania was launched which stresses the role of the private sector in mineral sector development. The policy specifies the role of government as that of regulating, facilitating and promoting the sector. Also in April 1998, a Bill for a new Mining Act was passed in parliament and approved by the President in July. Regulations to support the Bill have been prepared and circulated for comments to government departments and institutions and to stakeholders. They were scheduled to be finalized in December 1998.

The new government policy has attracted many companies to register and operate in Tanzania. These include the Ashanti Goldfields, Anmercosa, Kahama Mining Corporation, Afrika Mashariki Gold Mines (in Tarime), Pangea Minerals, Tanganyika Gold Mines,

Arusha Planters and Traders. Others are the Golden Pride Project (in Nzega), Bulyankulu Gold Mines, Golden Ridge (in Shinyanga) and many others. The government expects that by the year 2000 the mining operations of most of these mineral companies will have substantially increased.

It is estimated that, during the next four to five years, the mining industry will be producing over 15 tons of gold worth USD 140 million at today's prices (Kizigha, 1998).

The mining industry is no doubt contributing to the national economy. An example of the 1997 exports is given in Table 15 below:

Table 15 Examples of Exports of Precious and Semiprecious Stones for 1997 (in tons)

Commodity	Quantity
Various precious and semiprecious stones (excluding diamonds)	104,765
Dust and powdered diamonds	-
Diamonds	- -
Gold including gold plated with platinum	49

Source: Bank of Tanzania (1997)

Observations in Geita and Kahama indicate that where the mining companies operate, they are contributing to the improvement of the socioeconomic infrastructure and thus benefiting the local communities. For example significant contributions are being recorded in the areas of roads, schools, hospitals, water and power. In addition the industry is becoming a significant source of employment. It will, however, be important to carefully research, document and follow up on the contribution of the sector to all these different aspects.

However, the biggest concern relating to the growth of the mining sector is the issue of environmental degradation. These developments need to be carefully regulated in order to minimize the impacts on the environment. The extraction, processing, smelting and refining of minerals all have environmental implications. For details of the various implications of the mining industry see Nyanyaro (1990).

The government realizes the environmental implications

associated with the development of the mining industry and is insisting that mining activities have to be preceded by an Environmental Impact Assessment. But legislation to enforce this requirement has yet to be enacted. It is crucial that this is finalized as soon as possible because it is most likely that pressure is likely to mount, even on protected areas like the Serengeti National Park where there are reported mineral deposits.

Implications of trading on the natural resource base

We have seen in the previous section that trading on the natural resource base has many implications. We have already raised the question of the sustainability of some of the traded commodities. This issue is particularly pressing in wildlife trade. We have noted that there is illegal trade on some Appendix One animals, such as chimpanzees and elephants. But even for those commodities, which are legalized, there are many indications that traders do not adhere to the rules. All these points will be made clearer later in this section.

For some commodities, however, like minerals, the main issue is the environment. Enforcement of the policies is so far ineffective because some of the instruments, like Environmental Impact Assessment, are yet to be backed up by legislation. But even more so, there is no framework environmental law. The process towards achieving this objective in progress and we hope that it will be completed before too long.

As mentioned above, there are various mechanisms in place to regulate trade based on natural resources. These include policies, legislation, quota systems and international surveillance groups. The last two are more relevant to the wildlife trade. Let us look at each of these in turn:

Policies and legislation

We saw in the previous section that many animal species are traded. They include reptiles (snakes, crocodiles, tortoises, etc.), birds, mammals, amphibians and fish. Some of these are covered by specific policies, such as live birds, crocodile and ostriches. Others, however, are not.

These international and national policies help to regulate the wildlife trade. The Wildlife Department of the Ministry of Natural Resources and Tourism deals with CITES and other aspects of wildlife trade. The CITES Management Authority is also responsible for CITES plants and timber issues. The Fisheries Department controls the fish trade. There is however a notable lack of strict implementation of the approved policies and legislation.

The ability of the Wildlife Department to manage wildlife populations and enforce legislation related to trade, is a crucial point. The point has attracted a lot of debate, both at local and at international level. Where as the department is trying its best, other stakeholders feel that the control is not effective, despite the existence of legislation. The ineffective enforcement of the wildlife legislation and the related policies, has been an area of much concern for a long time.

It is alleged that there is a general lack of will to enforce the existing legislation. The factors relating to this unwillingness would be an interesting but important area of research. Many questions need to be answered if effective strategies have to be put in place. For example is this 'lack of willingness' to enforce policies and legislation a way to cover up malpractice? Or is it a lack of capacity to interpret and enforce them? Could it be that the problem is inherent to the faulty institutional structure, where responsibilities are so spread out that at the end of the day no one is responsible?

International surveillance groups such as NGOs, CITES and TRAFFIC have expressed their concern about this ineffective control of the wildlife trade. Dealers of export commodities have been unscrupulous to the extent of forging documents. Occasionally these forgeries have been uncovered. For example, in 1992, the CITES Secretariat discovered forged documents issued in Tanzania. CITES alerted other parties not to accept any CITES permits and the corresponding shipments of live specimens from Tanzania without cross-checking with the secretariat for confirmation of authenticity (1995). The names of the Tanzanian dealers were listed on the notice. But nobody knows what further action was taken. In 1995 CITES also noted anomalies in the export of live birds and it recommended the suspension of imports of five bird species, the leopard tortoise, pancake tortoise, and the Kenyan Sand Boa.

The above examples suggest that the problem of ineffective control and the forgery of export documents is much more widespread. Apart from policies and legislation, the other mechanism for controlling the wildlife trade is the quota system, the subject of the next sub-section.

The quota system

The quota system allocates the species and the numbers to be traded in a particular year. At the moment fish, plants, and timber are not included in the quota system. It is foreseen that in future they may need to be included and that they may need to come under national and CITES control.

There are many problems related to this system. Number one is the question of facilitating it. Second is the issue of the pressure exerted by the commercial sector, which consequently undermines the implementation of the system.

The 1994 quota came about as a result of the Planning and Assessment for Wildlife Management (PAWM) project facilitating the dialogue between individuals, groups and other interested parties. The 1994 quota was a compromise that balanced requests from the commercial sector and the knowledge on the biology of the potential exports and conservation (Howell, 1995). The question that arises here is what happens if no institution or individual take the initiative to facilitate the process of coming up with a quota. Are we going to see the end of the system? If not, what institutional mechanisms are in place to ensure that the system does not come to a halt?

The Bird Trade Workshop (Leader-Williams and Tibanyenda, 1995) also covered aspects of formulating the quota system. The principles are generally applicable to the entire live animal trade (birds, mammals, amphibians, reptiles, fish and invertebrates). But these and other principle require follow-up. And that is not all. The availability of biological knowledge is always taken for granted. But who is responsible for ensuring that there is a database which is continually updated so that data is available to form the basis for new quotas?

In the absence of good and up-to-date databases the quota system is bound to remain arbitrary. For example it is reported that the 1995 national quota was increased substantially without any scientific basis. New species were added with no information on their abundance (Howell, 1995).

150

Even the experiences from the 1994 quota were not used. These examples clearly demonstrate that the quota system is to a large extent influenced by the business community whose primary concern is to satisfy the market and maximize profits while the market is still there. Tomorrow may never come for them, so the concept of sustainability is of secondary importance.

Experience indicates that quota systems are poorly implemented. For example TRAFFIC has observed poor implementation of the 1994 quota. The quota specified 131 species and 95,400 individual animals through the Dar es Salaam exit between January and October 1994. But over 300,000 birds alone were actually exported during only a part of that period. When the figures for other groups of animals are added, the deviation from the quota is frightening.

It is not only that the quota numbers were deviated from, nine prohibited species were also given permits and 72 species not in the quota were exported (Howell, 1995). Furthermore TRAFFIC has also noted that 34 companies were initially issued with export licences for the 1993 stock. But in the end over 60 companies obtained permits for export of live birds. What is even more astonishing is that only 23 of them had a Trophy Dealer's License. This was clearly a contravention of the government's Bird Policy Paper.

It will be clear from the above that although the quota system is an important management tool, it has to be used along with other aspects of wildlife management.

Other potential research questions

Throughout the paper we have tried to suggest areas that could be the subject of research. In this section we raise more.

Normally natural resources are undervalued. This not only robs the source countries of revenue but also threatens the sustainability of exports and therefore potential revenue. Research could help to realistically value the various commodities traded so that at the end of the day there is a fair play.

While ensuring fair play it is equally important to relate wildlife trade to the issue of poverty alleviation. The economic value of genetic resources is increasing but the same cannot be said for the commercial value of any given species or extract. The same technological advances have vastly increased the supply of and demand of genetic resources. In the short term competition among firms for access to small numbers of quality suppliers will increase; over the long term the large supply of genetic material and the decreasing costs of natural product production are likely to hold the market value of raw materials very close to the direct labour costs of obtaining a sample (Reid, 1997).

Plants are being extracted by pharmaceutical companies without being valued properly. How do we change this situation?

We know that the custodians of the resources traded are the rural communities. It is important to look into how these custodians benefit or do not benefit from the industry. Preliminary studies suggest that local trappers of animals for trade for example get almost nothing. It is even worse when the community is put into the picture.

Ideally wildlife trade should provide a livelihood to the rural folk and exporters, as well as providing foreign exchange for the exporting nations. But we know that the profits from the wild bird trade go to middlemen and do not benefit the community or governments in exporting countries. Rural people who are the primary trappers of these birds receive the least economic benefit from this trade, ranging from 1%- 2% of the retail price of the birds (WCI, 1992).

It is therefore critical to look into who is actually employed in the trade, how many and how the revenue accruing from the trade could be ploughed back to benefit the local communities, management and even research.

The issue of sustainability also needs to be looked into. This is because the greatest tragedy of the wild bird trade and other animals is that more species are becoming endangered and, since there is no reinvestment of the profits into management, the issue of sustainability is called into question. It is important to look into ways of sustainably harvesting the resource base. It may be equally important to look into ways of promoting alternative economic options such as ecotourism.

Tanzania's policy on wildlife recognizes its importance to conservation and the need for sustainable utilisation of its wildlife resources for the benefit of the nation, most especially its rural population. The problem is that for a country as large as Tanzania, with so many wildlife species, there are few professionals who can guide efforts towards the sustainable utilisation of natural resources, particularly in the area of data and information provisioning. How can we best tackle this problem?

References

Bureau of Statistics (1989), Statistical Abstracts, 1987, Planning Commission, Dar es Salaam.

Bureau of Statistics (1997), *Statistical Abstracts, 1995,* Planning Commission.

Howell, K. (1995), *The 1994 Quota System,* Unpublished.

Kizigha, C. (1998), *Mining Sector Sees Light at the End of the Tunnel,* Feature Article, Daily News, No 28.

Leader-Williams, N. (1998), *The`Live Bird Trade in Tanzania,* Kakakuona, April-June, No. 9, p16.

Leader-Williams, N. & Tibanyenda, R.K. (1995), *Live Bird Trade in Tanzania: Proceedings of a Workshop held in December 1991,* Planning and Assessment for Wildlife Management, Department of Wildlife.

MNRT (1994), *Tanzania Forest Action Plan, 1994/95- 2007/08,* Unpublished.

Nyanyaro, T. (1990), 'Environmental Impact of Mining, Quarrying and Oil Exploration', in: Kauzeni, A., Kikula, I., Bitanyi, H. & Ngoile, M. (eds.), *Proceeding of the First National Workshop on the National Conservation Strategy for Sustainable Development for Tanzania,* held in Dodoma from 12-17 November, NEMC

Reid, W.V. (1997), 'Technology and Access to Genetic Resources', in: J. Mugabe, C.V. Barber, G. Henne, L. Glowka and A. La Vina (eds.), *Access to Genetic Resources: Strategies for Sharing Benefits,* ACTS Press, Kenya.

URT (1997), *National Biodiversity Country Study,* Unpublished.

WCI (1992), *The Wild Bird Trade – When a Bird in the Hand Means None in the Bush,* WCI Policy Report Number 2.

About the Contributors

Eduard Jansen, Member, RAWOO Secretariat

Juma Mwapachu, Lawyer, Member of the Governing Board, Society for International Development, Tanzania Ambassador to France

Joseph Semboja, Associate Professor of Economics and Executive Director, REPOA

Matthew Luhanga, Professor of Electrical Engineering and Vice Chancellor, University of Dar es Salaam

T. Ademola Oyejide, Professor of Economics, University of Ibadan, Nigeria

Brian van Arkadie, Formerly Professor of Economics, Institute of Social Studies, The Hague and University of Dar es Salaam

Samuel Wangwe, Professor of Economics and former Executive Director, Economic and Social Research Foundation

Flora Musonda, Senior Researcher, Economic and Social Research Foundation

Jenerali Ulimwengu, Sociologist, Journalist, Chairman Habari Corporation

Issa Shivji, Professor of Law, University of Dar es Salaam

Penina Mlama, Executive Director, Forum for African Women Educationists, Nairobi; formerly Professor and Chief Academic Officer, University of Dar es Salaam

Idris Kikula, Professor of Ecology and Principal, University College of Lands and Architectural Studies

Aida Kiangi, Formerly with the National Environment Management Council